I AM ME

Sharron Taylor

Dedication

To the Father, The Son, and The Holy Spirit.
You were my light in the darkness, my voice in the
silence, and my strength when I had none. This story
is a reflection of your mercy and grace.

To the woman I became.
You survived what should have destroyed you. You
chose to heal, to rise, and to speak. This is your legacy.

To my children.
You are the reason I fight. Every page of this book
carries your names between the lines. I pray my truth
gives you courage, and my love gives you wings.

"It is easier to build strong children
than to repair broken men."
— **Frederick Douglass**

Contents

PART IV: Becoming Me 93

PART V: The Final Out 105

Prologue

This book was inspired by the true events of my life, spanning from birth to age twenty-five. Though it may resemble an autobiography, I've chosen to classify it as non-fiction to protect the identities of those featured in these stories.

As I reflect on my past, I've come to realize how deeply traumatic many of my experiences were—and how they continue to shape the decisions I make every day. Even as a teenager, and now as an adult, I understand that my life has always been different. My childhood, my perspective, and most of all, my mind—are all uniquely my own.

I've never spent much time dwelling on the things I cannot change. After all, we don't get to choose our parents, our childhoods, or the families we're born into. And even if we could—who's to say we'd get it right? But reflecting on my life, I'm reminded that everyone carries a story. My siblings, for example, lived through many of the same events, yet would tell vastly different versions. One day, I hope to share their stories too.

I first drafted this story in 2012, at the age of twenty-three. I was pregnant with my third child, working as a security guard, and had only a high school education. I spent eight to twelve hours a day behind a desk, scribbling pieces of my past onto paper. I can't recall exactly what inspired me to start writing—but I did.

Now, more than a decade later, I'm revisiting these pages with two degrees behind me. Editing this book has proven difficult. Many memories have faded, buried beneath years of healing, distance, and trauma. In truth, I couldn't rewrite these moments even if I tried—and maybe that's for the best.

So, while this version of the book has been lightly revised, much of it remains as it was originally written—raw, unfiltered, and authentic to the voice of the 23-year-old woman who lived it.

I've been encouraged to tell my story by many: childhood friends who witnessed my struggles firsthand; people who follow my journey on social media, seeing mostly the highlights but little of the adversity; strangers who are shocked when they hear what I've endured; and professionals—social workers, psychologists, mentors, and nurse case managers—who've listened to me with empathy and care.

I have three hopes for sharing this book with you:

1. I hope it holds your attention from beginning to end.
2. I hope it inspires you to stay resilient and rise above your own challenges.
3. I hope that it encourages you to tell your own story—because once we're old enough, we become the authors of our own lives.

This is mine. And when you read the next chapter, I hope you'll understand just how far I've come.

PART I:

Surviving Childhood

CHAPTER 1

Be a Big Girl

Some nights, our mother would wake us up with whispers and tears—nights that started with panic and ended in silence.

"Kids wake up. John, Janice, Janette, wake up," she whispered at three a.m. on a school night. "Wake up, scoot over," she cried, breath thick with the smell of beer. "I'm dying. I'm about to die. I can't take it no more. I'm sorry I couldn't be a better mother."

She carried on like this for hours, tears streaming down her face. The three of us—my brother, my sister, and me—sat on the pull-out couch in that cramped living room, pleading with her, "Mommy, please don't die. We love you."

My name is Janette. I was ten years old. Fifth grade. My teacher's name was Mrs. Skipper. My sister Janice was seven. My little brother John was eight. We were living with our mother's friends Kristi and James—though "drinking buddies" might be more accurate. They had two kids too: Sheri, who was skinny like me with long, thin blonde hair, and Darwin, who had a blondish-brown, curly afro.

We all crammed into a small two-bedroom apartment in southwest Atlanta, just a couple of miles from Greenbriar Mall. The place reeked of cigarettes by day and alcohol by night. The three of us shared that pull-out couch, hoping this arrangement was temporary. Our mother lay beside us, but she didn't really sleep—at least not when she should have.

That particular night sticks in my memory. I was both terrified and annoyed. We went through this routine almost every other night. We were just kids—how were we supposed to handle it? I tried to act like I understood, so I could comfort Janice and John. I felt like I had to. It should have been our mother's job to protect us, but how could she when she was the one causing the harm?

I had to grow up fast. Too fast. That was the moment my childhood ended.

"I'm going to die; it's going to be ok though. I did the best I could. I'm so sorry," she continued.

Janice and John cried. I cried too, but I held them, tried to stay composed, told myself this was just another night. Soon, she'd wander off to cry to someone else—someone who might pity her, or help her feel better.

This wasn't the mother I thought I knew. I sat there, confused, and angry. Angry because I knew her words weren't true—or at least I hoped they weren't. Her tears, her apologies—they felt empty. I told Janice and John, "It's ok. Mommy's going to be fine. Go back to sleep, we have school in the morning."

Those were the longest nights. I was tired of the routine. Her breakdowns. Her sorry's. I was scared too scared she'd actually die one night, and we'd be left wondering why. What would happen to us?

I coped by pretending nothing was wrong. But the question lingered: How could a mother do this to her children—again and again—like it didn't matter? Apologies are meant to lead to change. Hers never did.

It felt like we were reliving her funeral every other night.

Imagine that—children, forced to mourn a mother who was still alive, over and over again. We didn't understand life or death. Right or wrong. We barely understood family. But God was with me. Somehow, I always knew what to say, what role to play. I was meant to be there for Janice and John.

It was time to be a big girl. I had responsibilities no child should bear. I was their anchor. But who anchored me?

Looking back, I was unaware, but God was with me. He was there when I had no one else.

Eventually, we moved in with my mom's best friend, Cherie. She lived in a townhouse with her son, Tyrell. Cherie treated us like family. Her place was just a few minutes from the apartment, but it felt like a different world.

Cherie drank too, but if she were an alcoholic, she could at least hold it together. We slept in Tyrell's room, on a pallet on the floor. Mom still drank heavily. Still cried. But now she poured her sadness out to Cherie instead of waking us up. Though sometimes, we could still hear her.

Don't get me wrong. My mother tried. She was a good mother—by day. She worked harder than any woman I'd ever seen. She was strong. At this time, she was newly separated from her husband, my stepdad, John Jones Sr. That was just one of her burdens.

She was independent, even though John was the breadwinner. It often felt like she was raising us alone. And maybe she was.

With hindsight, I wonder if she was bipolar. She was like two different people. Strong and capable by day. Weak and unraveling by night. A functioning alcoholic. That's what they call it—someone who keeps up with life's responsibilities but still drinks too much.

She used drugs occasionally, though I didn't learn that until later. She just wasn't herself—or maybe she was, and she just didn't know who that was anymore. She was lost. And this chaos was our normal.

I try to piece together how it all started, but my memory is fractured. Like trying to complete a puzzle with 8,637 pieces of one solid color.

So, I'll start where I can.

At the beginning.

CHAPTER 2

In the Beginning

June 11. Kankakee, IL. It was the summer of 1989. I imagine everyone was enjoying their summer, especially in Kankakee—beautiful that time of year. It's a small town just south of Chicago, and when I say small, I mean *country* small. Between this city and nearby Momence is where my mother grew up.

That day, my mother was in Riverside Hospital giving birth to her first child.

There were complications during delivery, and she feared the worst. Doctors and nurses rushed around frantically, shouting that the baby's heart was in distress and her blood pressure was dropping fast. She was rushed to the operating room for an emergency C-section. She was terrified. After nine long months, it was now possible she would wake up and not get to hold her baby.

But hours later, my mother awoke to a beautiful, healthy baby girl—me.

Despite the traumatic labor, I arrived strong and well. She named me after a dear friend who had passed away. I was twenty-two and a half inches long and weighed seven pounds, thirteen ounces. My skin was pale as cotton, and I was bald as the day was long. I was Janette Jones.

During the delivery, my mother's boyfriend at the time, Keith David, was there by her side. It was a terrifying moment for her, and thankfully she didn't have to go through it alone.

Now you might be thinking: boyfriend? Not the father?

Exactly. We didn't know who my father was. My mother had two possible candidates and went with the one that made the most sense at the time. It was either Eric Williams or Anthony Smith.

If it was Eric, I was the result of a steamy homecoming fling in a 1987 red Corvette, late at night, fogging up the windows on a dark country road. If it was Anthony, I would've been the product of a one-night stand between a young woman and a man who felt like a savior—but that's a story for another book.

And no, neither of these men were in the hospital room with her.

At some point in my life, I learned the truth—my birth father was Eric Williams.

We'll get to how I found that out later, but he was a handsome man. He was only nineteen at the time I was conceived, a year younger than my mother. I'm told I look just like him—about five foot eleven, brown hair that fell over his eyebrows, warm brown eyes, tan skin, pink lips, and a few freckles across his face.

Eric and his family were Jehovah's Witnesses. He and my mother conceived me on the night of his senior homecoming. They had the Corvette, the night, and a road all to themselves. But they weren't married, and my mother didn't know how to tell him she was pregnant. She feared his family wouldn't accept her—more importantly, they wouldn't accept *me*.

Months after I was born, she finally worked up the courage to tell him.

But by the time she did, it was too late.

Eric was dead.

It was all over the news. He had been riding his motorcycle when a semi-truck supposedly hit him. He was found dead on the side of the road, the only visible injury, a dent in the back of his head.

Something didn't add up.

A semi-truck strong enough to kill someone should have left more than just a dent. There should have been broken bones, bruises, something. The truth unraveled quickly. Eric hadn't been killed in a traffic accident. He had been murdered—by two police officers.

On the day of his death, those officers were chasing a group of bikers who had allegedly robbed a store. The bikers got away, leading them to a deserted country road. That's where they spotted Eric. He was in the wrong place at the wrong time. They followed him further down the road, cornered him, and beat him in the back of the head until he lost consciousness. Then they staged the scene to look like a hit-and-run.

They left him there, lifeless, to cover their crime.

His family, and my mother, were devastated. No one wanted to believe it. Eric was a good man—he'd never hurt anyone.

Because of their actions, a little girl would grow up without a father. That little girl was me.

They took him away from me before I ever had a chance to know him. He never got to hold me, teach me anything, or even see my face to know what he was leaving behind. I often wonder what kind of people could take a life like that—with no remorse, no thought about the ripple effect.

The loss took a toll on my mother. She had truly loved him. He was kind to her, and she believed he was the love of her life. And just like that, he was gone.

Maybe that's where her pain started—or maybe it had started long before.

She didn't have family to lean on. Her own mother had passed away when she was a child, and with her parents divorced and remarried to other people, she barely knew her biological father. Suddenly, she was left with no parents, no family, and no partner. Just her and me.

She never told Eric's family. She kept the truth to herself and decided to raise me alone.

She lived her life as a single mother. And that's where our story begins.

CHAPTER 3

For Better or Worse

Now that it was just the two of us, my mother did her best to move on. After receiving the news about what had happened to Eric, she left Kankakee and returned to Momence to try and rekindle her relationship with Keith. The three of us lived in a small, cozy one-bedroom apartment with a beautiful view of the river. That river was so peaceful and serene.

Only a couple of months after returning home, my mother discovered that Keith had been cheating on her. She ended the relationship immediately. That day was harder than most. I was spoiled back then—not by material things, but by love. Even though my mom didn't have the best upbringing, she had siblings. Three of her younger sisters, from her biological father's side, lived nearby. They adored me. My feet rarely touched the ground because someone was always holding or doting on me.

The day she broke up with Keith, everything seemed to crash at once. She was frustrated, tired, and overwhelmed. Unlike most days, I wouldn't stop crying—an hour straight and counting. She had done everything: fed me, changed my diaper, bathed me, played with me, rocked me. Nothing worked. In a moment of deep despair, she swore the devil was working on her. She began to think terrible thoughts—of drowning me in the river or throwing me in the dumpster—just to silence the cries.

She didn't want to do either, but she was at her breaking point. So, she placed me in my crib and walked out the door. She went to sit by the river, hoping to clear her head. Even from the distance, she could still hear my cries echoing across the water. After about fifteen minutes, the cries stopped. She was worried, but also hopeful that maybe I had cried myself to sleep—and thankfully, I had.

Living in that apartment alone became too much for her, so she moved in with her biological father, Scott Walker, and her three younger sisters. We stayed there for about a month before moving again—this time into a loft above my grandfather's building, located on the corner of Lafayette Boulevard and South Central in Momence. My grandfather used the building to rent rooms to travelers. My mother always spoke fondly of my great-grandfather, saying he was more of a father to her than anyone else had ever been. I wish I had real memories of him.

My mother was still young, still trying to live what she imagined a normal life to be—working, hanging out with friends, trying to find joy where she could. One of her friends was Felicity Stromar, a vibrant free spirit who kept my mother laughing and in the loop on everything happening in town. One evening, Felicity came bursting into the loft excited about a party her cousin Brandon was throwing. She insisted my mother come along—"All the fine men are gonna be there," she said.

So, my mom packed us both up, and off we went to the party. She took me upstairs where other children were playing, supervised by someone while the adults danced and mingled. That night, Felicity introduced my mom to two of Brandon's friends: Tony—a tall, handsome guy with fair skin—and John, who was tall, dark-skinned, and brown-eyed with a charming smile.

My mom was what they called a "brick house" back in the day—strikingly attractive. A mix of Black, White, and Cherokee Indian, she stood at five-foot-one with long, wavy brown hair dyed golden blonde. Her complexion glowed, her petite frame perfectly proportioned: 34-26-34. She radiated confidence and was fully aware of her effect on men.

Felicity tried to pair her up with Tony since they were both fair-skinned, but my mother had eyes for John. He was only eighteen, still in high school—two years younger than her—but he had a smooth fade, chocolate skin, and a smile that said everything without a word. Despite being unemployed and inexperienced, he had charm. And that was enough.

When John tried playing matchmaker by talking up Tony, my mom cut him off. "Tony's not my type," she said, stepping closer. "You are." That was all it took.

They spent the rest of the night talking and dancing. My mother knew she had to be upfront. She told him, "If you want me, you need to understand—I come as a package deal." He was confused, so she took him upstairs and introduced him to an eight-month-old me.

John picked me up, and at that moment, my mom said she and I both fell in love with him. Everything about that night felt right. Within weeks, they were sharing a hotel room—my mom worked there and got a free stay. He was there every night.

Two weeks later, she came to her senses. This wasn't sustainable. She packed our bags and waited for him. When he returned, he found the packed bags and a woman ready to walk away. She told him she needed something real. Not a fling. Not a phase. A future—for me.

He dropped the bags, grabbed her by the shoulders, and said he wanted the same. Then he asked her to marry him.

A few days later, they were at the courthouse. My aunt Monique and her husband Raymond stood as witnesses. My mother wore a sundress; John wore slacks, a white shirt, and a tie to match. They were so young.

So in love.

So hopeful.

My mother found a hardworking, handsome man who loved both her and her child. And John had found a beautiful, independent woman.

They hadn't thought much about the future—just that they wanted it together. John's family lived in Chicago. His mother, Anna Mae, had once been a telephone operator. His father, Billy Jones, was a truck driver who died in a highway accident in 1977 when John was just five. Rumors swirled that Anna Mae and Billy's best friend, Marlon, had something to do with the crash. Not long after the accident, Bill's friend Marlon and Anna Mae married.

Despite the gossip, Anna Mae was a sweet woman. She welcomed my mother into the family with open arms, and soon after, my mom, John, and I moved to Atlanta to live with her and Marlon, whom John considered his father.

When we arrived, part of their house had recently burned down. My grandfather, mother, father, and uncle Shawn rebuilt it together. Anna Mae treated me like her own grandchild. I never questioned my place in the family.

As I grew, my personality blossomed. I hid my bottle in strange places just to yell "Bottle! Bottle!" and make the family find it. I spent hours with my cousins, especially Christy, Uncle Shawn's daughter, who was close to my age.

At two years old, I started singing. My grandfather would sit at the bottom of the stairs and announce, "Introducing... Miss Sharon Taylor!" in his deep, booming voice. I'd strut down, shy smile and all, and sing. The whole family clapped. My mom called me her little star. One day at the grocery store, she asked what I wanted to be. I lifted my chin and said proudly, "I'm going to be a superstar." She laughed—but she also believed me.

From that moment, she became my vocal coach, pushing me to sing properly, from my stomach. She wouldn't let me sing off-key all day. I had natural talent—if you ask me.

By then, John and my mom had been married nearly two years. He followed in Marlon's footsteps and became a truck driver. But he was changing. The sweet, charming boy was becoming a man—a controlling one. Much like Marlon. My mother didn't know that Marlon had been abusive for years. Men don't usually reveal that part of themselves upfront. She brushed off John's behavior as typical male dominance. She didn't know better. It was all trial and error.

After two years with my grandparents, my parents decided to have a child together. John had been a good father to me so far, and my mom was excited to share a pregnancy with a supportive husband. This time, she wouldn't go through it alone.

But reality set in early. John was always on the road—and he was cheating. Three months into the pregnancy, my mother was diagnosed with pelvic inflammatory disease (PID), likely contracted from his infidelity. It posed a risk to both her and the baby. She confronted John, who denied everything. They argued often, but she didn't want to fight anymore.

Then it got worse.

One night, during an argument in their upstairs bedroom, my mother walked out. As she turned her back, John shoved her down the stairs. She was five months pregnant—and already high risk. Family members called 911. She spent days in the hospital, unsure how to escape. She had no job, no money, one child, one on the way, and no family nearby. So, she stayed, praying things would change.

On July 8, 1991, she went into labor. After hours of labor, she gave birth to a silent, blue baby. He didn't cry. The room panicked. But when the doctor tickled his foot, he let out a loud wail. Relief swept the room.

That day, I met my little brother: John Robert Jones Jr. Six pounds, thirteen ounces, and full of life. His eyes changed color with his mood, and he was absolutely beautiful.

After a few more months at John's parents' house, we moved into a small white house on Washington Road. It was our first real home as a family of four. But living alone didn't make things easier, it made them worse. John became more abusive, sometimes even in front of us.

After five months, something happened, something bad enough that we had to move back in with my grandparents. My mother loved them, but living there again weighed heavily on her. She hated how her mother-in-law stirred up trouble between her and John. She seemed constantly stressed.

Looking back now, I wonder: if she was so unhappy, why did we ever return?

CHAPTER 4

Finding a Way Out

After only being back a month, Anna Mae had already started pressuring our parents to have another child. Despite her doubts, my mother found herself pregnant for the third time. She was skeptical from the beginning—she knew the kind of relationship she had with John. He was always working, and when he was home, he was either drunk or abusive. Still, she gave in.

Don't get me wrong, John was a good father in some ways, even if I can't recall anything specific he ever did for me. But the truth is, he was abusive, and I believe he genuinely thought that was what being a husband meant. He had been beating my mother since she arrived in Atlanta, and he continued through her third pregnancy.

On December 5, 1992, early in the morning, my mother went into labor. She had planned to name the baby Smooth Willie Jones after John's father, Lucky. But to her surprise, the doctor delivered a baby girl.

When my mother woke up from her C-section and held her daughter for the first time, she began to cry—she was that beautiful. At five pounds, she was her smallest baby yet. My mother hadn't prepared for a girl and hadn't even thought of a name. So, she named her Janice Jones. She was a caramel-colored baby with big, beautiful black eyes, chubby cheeks you wanted to kiss all day, and a head full of black curly hair. She completed our family. We were all so excited to have her.

A few months after my mother recovered, we finally moved out of John's mother's house. With three kids, my mom knew it was time to have her own space again. After a house hunt, they found a beautiful blue home on Avon Avenue in southwest Atlanta, just 10–15 minutes from my grandparents' house. It was right off Cascade Road, near where Tyler Perry later filmed his Madea movies. Back then, of course, it wasn't his. But this was a great starter home—better than the first.

Once we had settled in and got furniture, my mother began inviting friends over. One friend in particular started visiting more than she was welcome. Her name was Tiana, and she brought her two children, Tahlia and Draya, with her. Tiana was loud, ghetto, and downright trifling. Oh—and did I mention she was our godmother? Yeah... so.

She and my mother would drink, smoke, and laugh loudly as they vented about their men. Meanwhile, the five of us kids would stay in our room playing with our toys. By then I was six, JJ was four, and Janice was three. We had a ton of toys. I owned every Barbie you could think of, and Janice had every baby doll ever made. JJ mostly played with us—sometimes with G.I. Joes.

After our mom and Tiana got good and drunk and their high started coming down, Tiana would leave with her girls. That's when our mother would come check on us. One night, she walked into our bedroom and saw it was a complete mess—nothing was torn up, but everything was out of place. She was upset and told us to clean up immediately.

Even at six, I had a controlling streak and liked things done my way—which, of course, I thought was the right way. My siblings weren't helping. Janice and JJ would just throw toys around and call it "cleaning." So I'd make them sit down and let me do it myself. I got that from my mother—she was always fussing about doing things right the first time.

Kids are smart, and I quickly learned how to avoid trouble by mimicking her.

My mother's way became my way: clean it once, clean it right. I knew better than to do a half-asked job and risk her coming back in and making us start over. That usually involved yelling and whooping's.

That day, though, we must've taken too long. She decided we needed to learn a lesson. She said we didn't appreciate having a nice home or our own room. So, she packed each of our little "Going to Grandma's" bags with a few clothes, filled up a couple more suitcases, and put us out of the house. She sat us on the front porch with our bags and said, "Don't cross that street, and don't leave the yard."

It was clearly a scare tactic, but we were too young to understand that. I tried to be the leader. I stood in the yard, desperately trying to come up with a plan. I thought about going across the street to ask our neighbor for help. She was an older lady and very kind. But I couldn't cross the street—I'd been told not to. JJ and Janice were crying, completely confused about why we were outside in the first place. I don't think we learned any real lesson that day. I just remember being so frustrated that the only plan I could come up with—going to the neighbor's house—was impossible unless I could fly.

Eventually, our mom let us back in. I don't remember much after that. So, moving onto the next tragedy.

It wasn't long before the beatings started again. This time, he didn't care if we saw it. He never tried to hide it from us.

As I got older, I learned more about John's upbringing and began to understand where his behavior came from. I wish my mother had had the courage to leave him sooner, but I know that would've changed a lot of things. She made another attempt to leave, but the same questions haunted her: where would she go? How would she survive?

It was a cycle—get beat, think about leaving, be too scared, and stay. She kept choosing to stay, praying for strength to endure whatever came next.

And then it got worse.

John began turning his rage on JJ and Janice. I guess the only "blessing" I had was that I wasn't really his child. JJ was five the first time it happened. He'd been potty trained since he was two and never wet the bed. But one night, he must have had too much to drink before bed and had an accident.

Our mom was working, so it was just us and John.

He came into the room, yanked JJ by the arm, and threw him in the bathtub. After cleaning the bed, he returned, pulled JJ out of the water—soaked, cold, and shivering—and beat him with a thick black leather belt until he bled. He screamed at him never to pee in the bed again, all while whipping his little body.

My sister and I could hear the screaming from our room. We cried too, wanting to help, but frozen in fear.

I couldn't wait for our mother to come home. I knew the marks wouldn't fade quickly, and I hoped she'd finally leave. She was furious when she saw what he had done, but even that wasn't enough. She threatened that if he ever hurt one of her children again, she would kill him. I'm not sure if he believed her, but something about that stuck.

Still, she continued to endure his abuse.

One night, John came home drunk, ranting, and raving. We heard them fighting in the dining room. We ran in to find him with his hands around her throat. He was choking the life out of her. She fought back, and he slapped and punched her for it. We stood there helplessly, crying, watching him torment her.

Eventually, she broke free and left. It wasn't safe to drag us out at that time of night, so she left us there. We ran back to our rooms, terrified.

Our parents had two friends, JT and Niki. JT was a drug dealer and one of John's suppliers. Niki was his wife and a friend of my mother's. That night, my mother showed up at their house, battered and shaken. Niki wasn't home, but JT let her in. He gave her a blanket and an alarm clock and let her sleep on the couch.

The next morning, John showed up at JT's for more drugs—and saw my mother. He immediately became violent, beating her again and choking her, saying she should call her father to say goodbye.

Shaking, she called Grandpa Scott and gave him the phone. John took the phone, listened for maybe 45 seconds, then quietly handed it back and walked out the door.

To this day, only he and Grandpa Scott know what was said. But it was enough. That day, my mother came home, packed all her things—including ours—and we left. We moved back to Momence, into the same loft owned by my great-grandfather.

Within days, my mom had three jobs and was back on her feet. Two weeks later, John began calling. He wanted to see us.

Uncle Jess—Mom's half-brother—was living with us at the time. I was eight, JJ was six, Janice was five. My mother didn't want to be bitter. Though they were separated, she wasn't ready to divorce him. She hoped, again, that things might change. So, they made a deal: if he wanted to see us, he had to take all four of us for two weeks and return us afterward.

We called our mom every day. We cried, but we got in trouble for that. When the two weeks ended, Mom grew concerned. He hadn't reached out. I overheard their phone call that night—him telling her she needed to come get "her damn kids" because his girlfriend was coming over and he needed to cook for her.

My mom showed up that night, furious. John tried to act tough, but she punched him square in the mouth. To everyone's shock, he did nothing. She told him she was taking her kids and leaving—for good. She warned him not to bring another woman into her house.

That night, she calmed down, packed our bags, and made us dinner. We slept there, but she didn't. She was probably wide awake all night, waiting for someone stupid enough to show up. No one did.

The next morning, we went home to Momence. A few weeks later, John started calling again, begging her to come back. She was still torn. Instead of divorcing him like she knew she should, she made one final compromise.

If he wanted to be with her, he had to move to Momence.

She told him she wasn't starting over again—she was finally doing well. She had rediscovered a piece of herself, and she was putting herself first.

And just like that, John moved back to Momence.

CHAPTER 5

The Truth

Once he got to Momence, he and my mom were doing fairly well—at first. But it wasn't long before our grandfather found out she had let him move in with us. He reminded her of the conversation they had over the phone that night at LC's and told her that as long as he was living there, we were not welcome. He put us out.

Eventually, my mom and dad found a house on Third Street. It was a big blue two-story home with a sizable front yard and an oversized backyard filled with mulberry bushes and honeysuckle trees. They planned to stay a while and even enrolled us in school. I was in third grade, and I remember walking to the bus stop in my snowsuit, snow reaching up to my chest.

But before long, normal returned—and for us, "normal" wasn't good. Everyone moved in. It felt like a shelter. Our mom, dad, me, my sister, my brother, Aunt Monique, Uncle Ray, Granddad Scott, two dogs, a cat, a fish, and a bird. The house was crowded and chaotic. Every adult there was using drugs or drinking heavily. It was practically a crack house, though we didn't know what that meant back then. Cocaine, pills, alcohol, they consumed it like it was candy. And my mother had joined them.

My dad returned to the same destructive path he'd followed in Atlanta. Maybe my mother was too comfortable or too afraid to leave, but either way, life for us became unbearable. Despite everything he had done, including cheating on her with her sister—she stayed. I guess she was broken.

When the school year ended, it seemed like my mother's memory of his abuse had faded. They moved us back to Atlanta. As usual, we started out at our grandparents' home until our parents found another place. Soon we moved to the very last unit in Landrum Arms Apartment Homes.

By now, my mom had become a workaholic. I assumed she worked so much to avoid our father. After nearly nine years of marriage, she had mastered the art of dodging his abuse. Our parents were never home at the same time. When she was home, she was always sick. When he was home, he was drunk. The stress made her anorexic. And he only got worse.

One day, he beat my sister. I still don't know what she did. I just remember her running from him and him dragging her from under our bunk bed, holding her upside down, beating her with his belt. She screamed, her face turning red from the blood rushing to her head. I couldn't wait for our mom to come home so I could tell her. But when I did, she did nothing. She was just as scared of him as we were.

By then, she was planning her escape. She met a kind man named Darius Turow at work. He was always offering to help. One night, after another argument with our dad, she called Darius. He paid for her to stay in a hotel for the night.

The next morning, she returned to the apartment with Darius waiting outside, just in case. She left the front door open as she hurried to collect our things. Our dad was inside, drunk, and furious. We stood in the hallway, watching him pull her by the hair and throw her around.

I saw him throw her body down the hallway. I grabbed my sister just in time. Our mother hit the floor and slammed into the wall. She was unconscious for a moment. When she got up, she stumbled. He threw her onto the bed and tried to lock the door. We watched him from the hallway as he continued to beat her.

Then we heard sirens. Our upstairs neighbor had called the police. That was the last time we saw our father for a long time.

After that, Darius began staying over more often. He and Mom slept on the two couches pushed together. Though she hadn't finalized the divorce yet, they were growing closer. But the old apartment had too many bad memories. Plus, my mother had her own trauma with mice, and our neighbor was sharing them with us through the laundry room connection. That's when we moved in with her friends Kristi and James—the same place I wrote at the beginning of the book.

Night after night, the same scenes repeated. I noticed a little progress thanks to Darius, but the divorce was wearing on her. Then came the secret.

One night, she handed me a picture of her and me. Next to me stood a shadowy figure.

"Do you see the shadow next to you?" she asked.

"Yes," I replied.

"I believe that's your father. John Jones is not your biological dad. Your real father was killed when you were a baby."

I was stunned. She explained that she'd been feeling haunted by the truth and felt it was time I knew. I wasn't angry. The picture was proof enough. She told me she'd contact my biological father's family so they could tell me more.

Eleven years after his death, she reached out. Despite their initial shock, they were thrilled to learn he had a child. They arranged for me to visit them that summer. While I finished out the school year, Darius paid for us to stay in an efficiency. My mom started working for the city and seemed to be finding herself again.

In March 2001, her divorce was finalized. She and Darius married a month later. It was a beautiful hunter green and white wedding, held in a church on the southwest side of Atlanta. All our family came—a surprise, considering we barely knew we had one. It felt surreal.

Before the wedding, we moved into a duplex on Mableton Parkway. It had almost six rooms on the first level. But, one month in, things soured. A woman named Kelly lived in the house behind ours. My mom started going over there a lot. She'd come back high, drunk, or both. I always knew—even when she tried to hide it.

Despite being newlyweds, she and Darius were already falling apart. She spent more time at Kelly's and less time being a mom. I missed the version of her that had started to come back.

Then came the trip that changed everything. The summer with my grandparents.

CHAPTER 6

Vacation

My mother and I drove eleven long hours to Momence, Illinois, to meet my grandparents for the first time. Their house sat at the end of what felt like a never-ending country road, surrounded by silence and space. For a city girl like me, peace felt foreign—almost eerie.

The house was small and white, with cacti scattered across the front yard and the biggest backyard I'd ever seen. It looked like it stretched a mile. The first portion was filled with fruit trees and vegetable gardens. Further back, there was a large homemade pond, and behind that, more open land. Beyond their property, a neighboring farm stretched into the distance. I loved everything about it.

Their home was beautiful. They even owned the house next door, which they rented to a kind family. That house was slightly larger and just as wooded. Later, I learned those trees weren't just for privacy—they hid a homemade go-kart track that my grandfather and my Uncle Benny had built together. Uncle Benny was the oldest of my grandparents' four children.

When we arrived, my mother walked me to the door. A tall white man with glasses and slightly yellowed teeth opened it— Benny Williams, my grandfather. Behind him was a short, beautiful woman who looked part Spanish, part Native American. Her name was Lucinda, my grandmother.

The moment they saw me; their eyes filled with tears. Any doubt or suspicion they may have had disappeared the second they looked into my face. My grandmother cried. She said I looked just like their son—the son they'd lost. For a moment, it was as if he'd come home. I felt the same way. Until then, I hadn't known what it was like to feel a part of something. Growing up, family only came around for holidays. This was different. This was belonging.

A day after settling in, I met Uncle Benny Jr., my father's older brother. He showed me the backyard, both houses, and took me to the shed where the go-kart was stored. I didn't believe the track was real until we rode it together. I hadn't felt that much fun since my tenth birthday party.

My first week there was full of adventure and discovery. I picked fresh fruits and vegetables straight from the yard and even tasted cactus my grandmother cooked herself. It was surprisingly good, especially with toast and a little salt and pepper.

Not long after, my grandparents planned a special trip to introduce me to more of my father's family. First stop: California, to meet my Aunt Marlene. We traveled in their RV, crossing state after state. I didn't know what part of California we landed in, but it was breathtaking. There were trees, water, and beauty everywhere, nothing like Atlanta.

My Aunt Marlene was petite and stunning, with long brown hair. She reminded me of what I might look like when I got older. She even looked like my father in the old pictures they showed me. She was married to a kind Spanish man who worked most of the time but always brought me something when he came home.

We only stayed a week, but every moment was special. They took me to the Pacific Ocean, where the clear blue-green water was cold and sticky against my skin. Though it looked shallow, the waves knocked me over the moment I let my guard down. It was my first taste of saltwater—literally. After that, I didn't go in too deep. The fish nibbling at my toes reminded me that somewhere in there, sharks were lurking.

After a shower and a change of clothes, we kept exploring. The next day, my uncle brought home a huge box of mangoes. I ate them until my stomach hurt. I had one once before, but this was next level. That same week, my aunt took me to Michael's and taught me how to make wreaths and holiday decorations. I made a few things for my mom to hang at home. We capped off the visit with a trip to the pool near her loft—where I discovered the joy of a Jacuzzi.

Leaving California was hard. I didn't want to go. For the first time, I felt like I was living the kind of life other kids talked about.

Next stop: New Mexico, to meet my Aunt Gloria.

Along the way, we made several stops. At one breakfast diner, I ordered rice pudding thinking it was tapioca. It was awful. I had a similar disaster with Tabasco sauce that night. Lesson learned: read the labels.

We finally arrived at Aunt Gloria's house, a red-and-white home in what looked like a desert. Heat waves shimmered off the ground, and cacti dotted the dusty yard. But inside, it was beautiful. The furniture was elegant, and everything felt new to me.

Aunt Gloria looked a lot like Marlene in photos, but now she was fuller, more mature. She was married and had two children, one heavier, one skinny as a beanpole. They were both younger than me, and we played together every chance we got.

She took me sightseeing and even bought me a new outfit—lime green and denim, my favorite. I felt like a superstar. It was one of the nicest things anyone had ever bought for me.

But that last night in New Mexico turned sour. I'd been scratching my head all day, thinking maybe I just needed to wash it. In the shower, I ran my fingers through my hair and saw tiny black bugs crawling under my fingernails. I was horrified. I kept scratching until I couldn't take it anymore, then tied my hair up and went to bed—silent, scared, and ashamed.

I didn't tell anyone.

The next morning, we said our goodbyes, and I rode quietly, itching and dreading what came next. All I could think about was telling my mom so she could fix it. The long ride back to Illinois gave me time to reflect, to calm my nerves. When we returned, my grandparents began teaching me about their faith. They were Jehovah's Witnesses and attended Kingdom Hall often. Though some beliefs differed, the core values resonated with me. Faith, family, discipline, I respected it.

A week later, my mom returned—this time with my little brother and sister. I knew something was wrong. She hadn't come just to pick me up—she had no plans of going back. Whatever happened in Atlanta had driven her to start over, again.

We stayed a week or two longer, and my mom even began attending Kingdom Hall with us. But just as we started finding our rhythm, it fell apart. My grandparents told us we had to leave. At the time, I didn't understand. I blamed my mom, thinking maybe we'd overstayed our welcome. It wasn't until later in life, around 2021 that I found out why we left and that this man was probably also not my father.

My grandmother Anna Mae had called them. She told them lies about my mom, and said she was using them for money, manipulating the situation. It wasn't surprising. This was the same woman who married her dead husband's best friend. But hearing it still hurt.

With nowhere else to go, my mom found the first house she could. It was a large blue house on the corner of two streets, with a huge living room and a full basement. She turned that house into a party zone. Her cousins Trish and Tyrone were always around, bringing a parade of shady people with them. The house reeked of liquor, weed, and chaos.

My siblings and I stayed tucked away in the basement while people upstairs danced around stripper poles, red lights flashing from the ceiling, and God-knows-what happening on the floors. I hated it. It was loud, dangerous, and nothing like the life I had glimpsed just weeks before.

Eventually, things slowed down—but only because my mother spiraled further. Tyrone introduced her to someone named Bobby White. He was tall, slim, with braided black hair and a charming face. He was 21—only six years older than me and thirteen years younger than my mom. Still, they got involved quickly.

Before long, Bobby was staying over regularly. That's when the real instability set in. We bounced from house to house, from friend to friend, sometimes living in cramped efficiencies, other times in cheap motels. It felt normal to me by then—constant motion, never settled.

But behind the scenes, things were getting darker. My mom started using harder drugs. She was overwhelmed, spiraling, and losing control. Eventually, she called our dad and asked if he could take us for a while.

He agreed.

And just like that, our lives changed again.

Top of Form

Bottom of Form

PART II:

Breaking
The Cycle

CHAPTER 7

Second Time Around

Our dad had already remarried—to the woman he cheated on our mom with. Or should I say, one of the main women he cheated with. Her name was Tasha Mcintyre, now Tasha Jones. They had a two-year-old son named Brandon. Tasha was a security officer for APS schools, and she didn't like the fact that my father had other children. She especially didn't like that we would be living with them, even temporarily.

But Tasha wasn't completely naive. She knew that if we came to stay, she could make use of us—especially me, since I was the eldest. When we arrived, our mom had already enrolled us in school. It was the beginning of the school year. I was in eighth grade, my last year of middle school at Bunch Middle School. My siblings were still in elementary school.

Looking back, I realized things were more confusing for them than they were for me. They didn't fully understand why we were there. After living with this man during our parents' marriage—a long, painful twelve years—we were all afraid of him. We feared being yelled at or beaten. He was unpredictable and angry. But we knew we had to stay.

Before we left, our mom explained that she needed us to go with our father for a while. It would only be temporary, she said. She needed time to get things together so we could live comfortably. We begged and pleaded, but there was no changing her mind.

At first, it wasn't so bad. We had our own rooms, and for the first time, I had my own space, my own bed, TV, and a little privacy. But things quickly grew uncomfortable. We walked on eggshells, afraid to be ourselves. We didn't eat much, bathe much, play, or even talk much. Staying outside was the best option.

As we adjusted to the neighborhood, we started going out more and eventually met other kids. I started playing basketball in the cul-de-sac and got pretty good—terrible on offense, but I was unbeatable on defense. I even thought about trying out for the school team.

When I asked my dad if I could try out, he said yes, and I was thrilled. But after a week of practice, I didn't make the team. The coach said it was because of my asthma, but I didn't believe him. It broke my confidence. Later, I realized that my dad had probably only said yes because he assumed I'd fail.

Still hopeful, I tried out for the soccer team and made it. I even took team pictures. But when I told my dad, he made me quit. I was devastated. I assumed then that he never intended to support anything I enjoyed.

Meanwhile, my siblings didn't have extracurricular activities. Tasha began using me to take care of Brandon. I became his primary caregiver. Every day after school, she'd pick us all up, and then I'd get Brandon out of the car, bathe him, help him with the potty, feed him, and put him to bed. She did the bare minimum.

Tasha put all her motherly responsibilities on me. Maybe it was tradition, or maybe she just didn't want to be bothered. Either way, I didn't care for her much. My siblings and I blamed her for taking our dad away, though I now know she wasn't the one to blame. Still, I hated doing so much for her.

Our dad hadn't changed. He was older, heavier, and still abusive. That Christmas was our first without our mother and our first with our father and another woman. We woke up excited, like every kid, hoping for gifts. The tree had been full for days. But we watched Brandon open nearly all the gifts. We each got three presents, and mine included oversized, off-brand sneakers that made me look like a clown. I was humiliated before I even wore them to school.

That night, we went to Grandma's house, as usual. Loud music, drinking, games, laughter, and cigarette smoke filled the air. Every room buzzed with conversation. As the night wound down, trouble began.

Our dad had been drinking all day. Tasha was ready to leave, but he wasn't. She started the car and told me to gather my siblings. Just as I was getting into the car, I saw him grab her by the neck. I grabbed Brandon and rushed my siblings back inside. People were crowding the doorway, and we were forced to watch him choke and beat her. Adults shouted at him to stop, but no one intervened.

I don't remember how it ended—just that it did. I was terrified. That night still haunts me.

A few weeks later, things seemed calm. Tasha's mother came to stay because she was sick. Earlier, at the grocery store, she had put back apples Dad wanted to buy. He didn't notice until later.

That night, while we were playing a board game, Dad came in looking for the apples. He exploded. He threw the board game, scattering the pieces. I grabbed my siblings, and we prepared to flee. He began beating Tasha again. Her mother begged him to stop.

Tasha's mom sent us out the door, telling us to get help. I carried Brandon while JJ and Janice followed. We ran to the neighbor's house, knocking quietly. I was terrified he'd see us. He stepped outside, looking for us. We ducked. Miraculously, he didn't spot us.

The neighbors finally answered. I begged them to let us in and explained what was happening. They took us in, and the husband called the police. When the blue lights arrived, we stepped outside, hoping we were safe. They didn't arrest him. Later, he came into our room and warned us never to leave or call the police again. We stayed silent, afraid.

Things got worse. We ate less and spoke less. Tasha always accused Janice of being greedy, which made her lose weight. When our mom called, we could never speak freely. Dad and Tasha listened to every word. Every time I heard her voice, I cried. I wanted to tell her everything and beg her to take us back. But I couldn't.

Despite her promises, I knew we'd be here for a while. I could tell our absence hadn't helped her. She was worse off. And I was scared. I didn't want to live like this—quiet, afraid, and unseen.

CHAPTER 8

May God Have Mercy

When the school year ended, my mom decided she missed us. Though she wasn't ready to take us back full-time, she planned to visit for a few days. She and Bobby had just gotten married at a courthouse in Kankakee and were now officially married. She was excited to share the news with us. She drove down from Chicago in her little gray car, barely big enough for five people, all the way to Atlanta.

Our dad dropped us off at our grandparents' house, and our mom picked us up from there. We went out for lunch and had a good time. We told her everything we hadn't been able to say over the phone. She was disgusted and upset by what we shared—but even that wasn't enough to change her mind about leaving us again.

Later that day, our dad called. We were all in the car, listening as she yelled into the phone. From what we heard, he told her she needed to keep her "damn kids." She shouted back, "Keep MY damn kids? John, I wasn't planning on keeping them! I was not prepared for this at all. I can't keep them. I've only been down here for a day! I don't have a place to stay, I'm not working—hello, John?!"

But her pleading didn't matter. Nor did her circumstances.

What I found out later in life was that his decision revolved around child support. He didn't want to pay while having us full-time. I understood it in a way, but still—it didn't change the fact that he left us with her, fully aware of her situation.

We ended up in a hotel for a few days. One thing about my mother—she always tried. She accepted the situation and began figuring out how we would live. Eventually, she reached out to an old friend named Bob from the Landrum Arms apartments. He owned a business and, thankfully, a few houses. With his help, we moved to Stone Mountain, Georgia.

We had nothing—no clothes, furniture, or food. But within days, we had enough. Most of our furniture came from street corners, but it was ours. We had a roof over our heads.

My birthday was coming up. I was turning fourteen and looking forward to starting high school. I hadn't had a real birthday party since I was ten, and I didn't expect one this year either. Still, we played baseball in the front yard, sang Whitney Houston songs, and even recorded a duet on a tape player. My mom bought me a cupcake and sang happy birthday. It wasn't much—but it meant everything. I was just grateful to be with my mom and alive.

At first, I didn't feel poor. But I started to notice signs that my mom was slipping back into drugs. She became more erratic. That's when I began staying with Mimi—my mom's adoptive mother.

Mimi lived off Cleveland Avenue with her youngest daughter Tanisha, who had Down syndrome, and her son Malik, who was addicted to crack cocaine. Also living in the house were two grandchildren whose mother was in jail, awaiting trial for allegedly killing their father.

Mimi didn't tolerate foolishness. If Malik didn't come home on time, she'd lock him out. Tanisha, however, would sneak him in while Mimi slept.

The first night I stayed, I had no pajamas. They gave me oversized pants I had to tie in the back just to keep on. I chose to sleep on the couch. Around 3 a.m., Tanisha let Malik in. I woke to a strange feeling at my feet. He was standing at the end of the couch asking me to scoot over. I told him I thought he wanted the bed, and he backed off, startled. I stayed awake until he fell asleep.

The next night, I chose the bed. Again, Tanisha let him in. This time, I woke to him tugging at my pants. I shot up, and he quickly turned around, pretending to watch TV. "What are you doing?" I asked. "Nothing," he stammered. "You know I wouldn't do anything to you. Okay?"

I was terrified—but afraid to say anything.

On the third night, I tied my pants in the front and slept with a kitchen knife under the cushion near my head. I pretended to be asleep when he came in—heart racing, every nerve on high alert. I opened my eyes and stared at him. He sat on the bed but didn't try anything. He knew I was awake—and ready. That night, I didn't sleep at all.

At 6 a.m., I got dressed and told Mimi I wanted to go home. She asked me if I wanted to stay another night, knowing how things were at home. But before she could even finish asking, I cut her off and immediately said I was ready to go. I just wanted to leave.

Back at home, I didn't tell my mom right away. But she could tell something was off. Later, I asked her to come upstairs. I told her everything.

She was furious. She called Mimi immediately. Mimi was heartbroken and disappointed that I hadn't told her sooner. But she didn't defend her son. She kicked him out.

Even though nothing had happened physically, I felt like something had happened. For a while, it became a bad memory I tried to forget. I never did.

But reality came crashing back. We couldn't get into the house one day—the locks had been changed. My mom, her husband, and the three of us spent the night on a cold concrete slab, probably eight by six feet. We huddled under blankets, trying to stay warm. I was embarrassed, scared of bugs, and afraid someone from school might see us.

The next day, we somehow got back inside. Bob must have given her a few days to get things in order, maybe thirty. But by October 2003, our time was up.

We had no place to go. So, we packed our clothes into a U-Haul and moved into a shelter near Metropolitan Parkway.

My mom enrolled JJ and Janice at the local school, but she didn't want me at Washington High. Mays High had a magnet program and offered free Marta cards for out-of-district students. I rode the #42 bus into downtown Atlanta, transferred to the westbound train, and caught a bus marked "Benjamin E. Mays."

It was a long, uncomfortable commute—especially in the Georgia cold, where mornings were freezing and afternoons sweltering. I didn't even have a coat. One morning, while waiting at the bus stop with my arms tucked in my shirt, an older woman who often rode with me gave me a forest green coat. It wasn't cute—but it was warm.

I was thankful but also embarrassed. No one at school knew I lived in a shelter. I did everything I could to hide it.

We spent Halloween, Thanksgiving, Christmas, New Year's, and Valentine's Day in that shelter. I hated it—but it was all we had. We slept on the floor of a sanctuary with about fifty people. Kids got cots. Adults got blankets. It smelled awful. But I was grateful we weren't outside again.

I tried to stay positive. I joined the church choir and a Christian youth girl group. Those girls became my friends. They didn't judge me, even knowing my truth. Their parents were ministers and professionals—nothing like mine. But they made me feel safe.

During that time, writing became my sanctuary. I wrote letters to God. Letters to my real father. Letters I never sent—just folded and kept. I wrote poetry and songs. It was how I coped. Once I wrote it down, it didn't feel like mine anymore. Writing kept me sane.

Watching my mom go through what she did made me vow to be different. I didn't want to be like her. I wanted to be strong, independent, and driven.

Because of her, I would become those things.

But as I watched her spiral, I no longer saw my mother. I saw a stranger—possessed by addiction. She had no self-control, no self-respect. And little by little, she lost the respect of everyone around her... even in her own home.

CHAPTER 9

First Love

There was one good thing I got out of living in the shelter—besides the knowledge of how to never go back—and that was my first love. When we first moved in, I learned the shelter was run by Dianna and her husband Richard. They had four biological children and two adopted ones.

Chris, the oldest adopted child, was tall and skinny with curly brown hair. Ashlin, the other, was a brown-skinned young woman with thick thighs and beautiful hair. She was rumored to have been the child of an addict and allegedly stripped before being adopted into this Christian family.

Their oldest biological child was Micah—short, slim, and cute with curly hair. He was a senior in high school, dating one of my friend's older sisters. The youngest was Celeste, two years younger than me but my height. We became best friends, along with Tiana (Ana) and her sister Camille (Cami), who also went to church there.

The child just older than Celeste was RJ. He was darker-skinned, slim like his siblings, and about 5'7". Dianna, their mother, was Italian—beautiful, kind, and sometimes a bit hard to read. She and her husband Richard, a handsome Black man, were not only the shelter owners but also pastors. They had one more child I hadn't seen at first. His name was Duke.

Duke stood about six feet tall, light-skinned, slim, with brown eyes and short hair. He had a baby face and, as I'd learn, a great sense of humor. I remember the first time I saw him: I was walking into the church after retrieving something from our U-Haul, and he was standing on the ramp with RJ. I felt an instant pull—love at first sight, maybe.

Even though I was nervous, I walked past them like I didn't notice anything. But I noticed everything. I didn't tell anyone how I felt at first. I'd never had a boyfriend, never felt this way before. I flirted at school, but this was different. He made me blush just by looking at me.

During Sunday service, I would scan the room for him. If we made eye contact, I'd quickly look away. Still, I noticed he began to show up more often, not hiding in the back office anymore. He made jokes, tried to make me laugh, and I could tell—he liked me too.

Eventually, I confessed to Celeste and Ana that I had a crush on him. They already knew and were excited I finally admitted it. Ana had a crush on RJ, which gave us even more to bond over.

Soon, the word spread and reached Duke. Celeste told me he felt the same when he first saw me but was afraid, I'd reject him. I never saw myself as a "pretty girl," so I didn't understand why he'd be shy.

With Celeste's help, we started talking. From that point on, we were inseparable. The counselors knew, our friends knew, even our parents knew. Duke was always around me. People who'd known him for years noticed a change—he stopped hiding and started glowing.

That Christmas, he asked me to be his girlfriend. I was over the moon. We started writing to each other in a shared composition notebook—swapping it weekly—and spent every weekend together. His mom supported our relationship at first, giving him the occasional reminder to be careful.

He never said he loved me, but I felt it. His sister told me he said he "almost" loved me. That was enough for me. Everything between us felt genuine, young, and innocent. We hadn't even kissed. He simply made me feel safe and cherished when I felt like I had nothing.

He believed in me when I didn't believe in myself. I saw myself as poor, skinny, unattractive—with addict parents, living in a shelter. But through his eyes, I was talented, kind-hearted, and worthy. His love sparked my ambition and reminded me that I was more than my circumstances.

I gave my life to God at twelve and prayed he'd pull us out of the darkness. I genuinely believed Duke was part of that answer. He was music to my soul—my love, my muse. I began writing more poetry, inspired by him. If love ever came again, I wanted it to feel like that.

I'll never forget one night when we were preparing for bed in the sanctuary. Families had their cots and blankets laid out. Duke stayed behind, sitting next to me on my cot until I drifted off. That night, he reminded me his love had nothing to do with where I lived.

In February 2004, we moved three doors down from the church. I was sad at first, thinking I'd lose Celeste, Ana, and Duke. But our new home was only a short walk away. A week later, it was Duke's birthday, and I bought him a hat—he loved wearing it. Then came Valentine's Day.

The church threw a party. Everyone was there. Suddenly, the room went silent, and I turned to see Duke walking toward me with a huge smile, holding balloons tied to a Hershey's bar and a card. My heart melted. He handed me the gift, and everyone stared. It was my first Valentine's Day surprise—and it was perfect.

The card said, "Happy Valentine's Day. I hope it's filled with all the little things that make you happy." He scratched out "little" and wrote "BIG (like me)" at the bottom. It was hilarious and sweet. I thought he might kiss me, but instead, he kissed my forehead—gentle, respectful, and perfect. Later he walked me to the blacktop to put my things in the car where he asked to have the chocolate he bought me. I thought it was cute and agreed.

Later, Duke's mom began expressing concern about our closeness. She didn't like my mom and thought we were too invested in each other. Dianna asked Duke to break up with me. He told me everything on the blacktop at sunset. I cried. But then he said we didn't have to break up. I was relieved.

But something shifted. We grew distant. I wasn't sure why, but I eventually thought maybe we should break up. Looking back, it was probably a mistake, but we were just kids. Weeks passed, and I missed him deeply. Celeste played messenger again, telling me Duke still loved me—he even called his mom by my name once.

Still, we didn't get back together. I grew angry and tried to provoke him. I let people think I was talking to two of his friends—Smoke and RJ. Smoke came around often, and though nothing happened, I let rumors spread. RJ, on the other hand, was immature and violent. Once, he threw a bottle at me, cutting my ankles.

Duke never said how he felt. And when I saw him flirting with another girl at church, I stopped going. He used to show love with actions, but now it felt like he was showing me he didn't care.

Eventually, it ended for good. I was heartbroken but grateful. Duke showed me what love could be. Even if I never saw him again, he'd always be one of the most important chapters in my life—and the standard by which I'd measure love forever.

CHAPTER 10

Bad Apple

Kenneth G. Ortiz once said, "Be wary of the company you keep, for they are a reflection of who you are—or who you want to be." It's not something we think about as children. Back then, I didn't see my reflection in the people I chose to surround myself with.

In May 2004, we moved again. By now, moving had become routine. We lived in three different houses before settling into a duplex off Cascade Road. That fall, I was enrolled at Frederick Douglass High School for my tenth-grade year. I didn't know anyone, but that didn't bother me—it wasn't my first new school, and it wouldn't be my last. I was used to starting over and had no problem making friends.

The person I connected with the most was Angel. She was tall, thin, brown-skinned, with short hair and a tough spirit. We discovered we had similar stories—addicted mothers, absent fathers, chaotic homes. It bonded us fast. Before long, she was spending nights at my house, and her younger sister even visited occasionally. Her sister and my brother JJ were in the same grade and even dated for a while.

My mother had taken in a disabled woman named Sylvia as part of a scheme to collect disability checks. Sylvia smelled like spit and urine, rarely bathed, and wore layers of filthy clothes. She was sweet underneath it all, and my siblings and I often found ourselves laughing with her. It was a strange setup, but my mom was surviving—hustling however she could.

Despite appearances, my mother hadn't changed. She had simply gotten better at hiding her addiction, or maybe we'd stopped noticing. She started acting more like an irresponsible older sister than a parent. She let us throw wild basement parties with drinking and no real supervision. It felt cool at the time, but looking back, we were far too young to be handed adult freedoms.

Eventually, we moved into the back of Bowen Homes, one of Atlanta's most dangerous housing projects. Known for its crime, drugs, and sky-high HIV rates, Bowen Homes was no place to raise a family. Still, we moved in with six dogs and two cats—one of them mine, a cat I named Mama.

Angel was still living with us and soon started dating my younger brother John. Despite their age difference—he was only fourteen—they ended up pregnant. In January 2005, Angel delivered a baby boy at just six months. He had no oxygen for twelve minutes and was declared unlikely to survive without severe disabilities. Heartbroken, she chose to remove him from life support. His name was Isaiah.

We collected donations in pickle jars to cover his cremation. People gave what they could, and we managed to cremate him in a blue and white flowered vase. That vase later became a point of tension between Angel and my mother.

After another move, Angel got pregnant again—this time with a girl, Esther. By then, our home life had spiraled into chaos. My mom had stopped parenting entirely. Angel and John were no longer together but still living under the same roof and still involved. The house became a revolving door for trouble. That's when I met Drake.

Drake was handsome and charming—at first. We spent a lot of time together until I realized he was lying, keeping both me and his child's mother in the dark about each other. After we broke up, I learned he had slept with my younger sister, Janice. I was disgusted and betrayed.

Then came the final betrayal: Angel started seeing Drake after I left. She lied to me about it for months. I had considered her a sister, and she betrayed me like that—just like she did to her own blood. I tried to give her the benefit of the doubt, but I couldn't ignore the truth.

The tension between Drake and John reached a boiling point when Drake pulled a gun on my brother, trying to rob him. Janice jumped in front of the gun, and John ran. Days later, Drake came back with a gun again. This time, my brother shot him in self-defense. The police couldn't prove anything until John confessed, afraid they'd arrest our mother instead.

Hearing that my baby brother had been arrested devastated me. I didn't want to believe Angel was involved—but she was. By then, she was pregnant again by Drake.

Eventually, I moved out and got my own apartment. Even then, I couldn't stop trying to take care of everyone. I let my sisters, my mom, and Angel move in. For four more years, I was the only one working, paying bills, and taking care of everyone—including my child, Seven. No one else even tried to contribute.

I begged God for a way out. I asked Him why my life wasn't changing, why I still felt stuck. And then it hit me: I was playing God in everyone else's life. As long as I kept enabling them, I would never grow. So, I made a plan. When my lease ended, they would all need to move out. It was the hardest choice I had ever made—but the most necessary.

My relationship with Angel was never the same. We drifted apart. I finally learned: you can't be the only good apple in a basket of spoiled ones. Eventually, the rot spreads.

CHAPTER 11

The Perfect Mistake

The last chapter was meant to show how two friends drifted apart, but it skipped over a lot of important details from my life. So, let's rewind a bit and fill in some of the blanks.

When we moved into the little tan house on Hamilton E. Holmes, life was already spiraling. Our house had officially become the "hood house." My mother had increased the Social Security/Disability income coming through our home by having so many people living with us.

There was this white couple, Sandy and his wife Mary, both on drugs. A Black man named Gary and his son came over daily. Mr. Bud, an older white man with diabetes, spent his time chain-smoking and eating honey buns. Then there was our grandfather, our two uncles who were six and seven, Sylvia (still with us), my mom's husband, Angel, her sister Erin, John, Janice, and me.

This was a four-bedroom house with a half-finished basement, barely big enough for two people—yet we were packed in like sardines. People didn't move in all at once, but even that doesn't make it better. Back then, I thought this was normal. It was just everyday life.

I was sixteen and starting to form opinions about my mother's husband. I didn't respect him; I blamed him for my mom's drug addiction. I hated them together.

Despite the chaos, I tried to maintain a sense of normalcy. I still got up every day and went to school—even if no one else did. School had become optional in our house. Most of us still went, but only because we wanted to.

I was in eleventh grade, still a virgin, and had only ever had one real boyfriend. I flirted a bit in tenth grade, but that was it. I was shy and cautious. But one day, all that would change.

Coming home from school, I saw a tall, brown-skinned guy talking to the neighbor's son. He was attractive, and I was sure he noticed me. I went inside, grabbed the phone, and called Angel—pretending to talk while standing outside, hoping he'd see me.

He approached. His name was T. He had short dreads and a nice smile. I asked to see his ID—he claimed to be 18, but the ID said 21. He insisted it was fake, just to get into clubs. I believed him.

We talked daily and saw each other every weekend. Eventually, he started coming by more often and staying late. Then the overnights began. Still innocent—mostly cuddling. But temptation crept in.

After weeks of pressure, I gave in—not because I was ready, but because I was tired of saying no. It was brief and painful. I immediately felt confused and guilty. I thought I loved him. He made me feel seen in a world where I often felt invisible.

A few days later, I told my mom. We were in the bathroom. "I lost my virginity," I said. Her response was surprisingly calm at first, almost excited. She asked me questions like when and with whom.

It went silent. She could sense that it wasn't the end of the story. Then I dropped the bomb: "I think I'm pregnant."

"You ain't nothing but a hoe! A stupid hoe!" she screamed. "Get out of my face!"

I locked myself in the bathroom. I didn't even feel mad at myself anymore. I just wanted to make a plan. I'd raise the baby with T. We'd be a family. Simple.

Back at school, I hid my pregnancy. I didn't want to become another stereotype. When I told T, he admitted the truth: he wasn't 18—he was 22—and he sold drugs. I felt betrayed, but I was naive. I didn't understand what had happened. That I had been groomed.

T sold drugs to my mom and her husband. I didn't realize then that he had intentionally gotten me pregnant.

Despite the red flags, I tried to hold the relationship together. I gave him a ring for Valentine's Day. He started working at a club, came home with the ring off or on the wrong hand. There were always "female friends."

Then one night, around 3 a.m., he showed up high. I let him in, and he started pacing. In the bathroom, he laid out lines of coke. I was stunned. He begged me to let him stay. I kicked him out.

That night changed everything. I couldn't be with him. I couldn't raise a child with someone just like the men I wanted to escape.

The summer came. I was five months pregnant. My sister was in seventh grade and thriving in cheerleading. But she couldn't escape the chaos at home. We spent our days outside playing cards, avoiding the madness.

June was rough. Asthma attacks hit hard. One night, I had to walk two miles to a payphone to call 911—T watched and did nothing.

By my seventh month, the attacks stopped. I was done with T. He didn't care about me or our baby.

Then our pets disappeared—sold for drug money. Sylvia spilled the truth. Bobby was using the pickle jar from Isaiah's funeral to panhandle again. My mom was spiraling.

My mom lived in an alternate reality where everything was fine. But we knew the truth—we were poor, neglected, and on our own.

God was my anchor. Through it all—feeling abandoned, betrayed, and overwhelmed—He was there.

Then came the breaking point. My mom screamed at us to get out. I ended up at T's house. His mom let me stay, but the situation didn't last. After a month or so I caught him talking to another girl outside and I knew then we were never going to work.

Heartbroken, I left and moved back in with my mom—now in a new house. She and her husband had divorced, and she had a new boyfriend. She had moved to Lakewood again. It was a house with a full basement, so it felt like we fit.

About 5a.m. on October 5th, I started experiencing the worst pain I had felt in my life. It felt like someone was grabbing every organ and muscle I had from the center of my spine and ripping it forward towards my belly button. They would ring it out, let it go, and three minutes later it would start all over again.

I went to my mom's room. She told me to lie next to her in bed as she counted the minutes between my contractions. They were three minutes apart, so we rushed to the hospital. My cervix hadn't dilated at all, so they sent me packing back home. I was miserable. They say hot baths help the cervix open, so I sat in the bathtub for hours.

Every three minutes for the next few hours I felt my body ripped to my belly button and rang out like a wash rag. I thought I would die. I would toss and turn in the tub getting water everywhere.

Finally, 10 hours later, we decided to go back to the hospital. They checked my cervix and still only ½ centimeters dilated, they sent me to the waiting room with no urgency to get me in my own room.

I hadn't eaten anything. I was going crazy. This pain was killing me. The nurses finally got me situated in a room and asked if I wanted an epidural. She explained how it worked, and I decided against it. I had been dying for the last 12 hours. I thought this baby should be coming soon and I never really like medicine. As 2 a.m. the next morning rolled around I had only reached 4 centimeters dilated. Still, I had been contracting every three minutes for the last 20 hours.

My mom, her boyfriend, and my grandfather were all at the hospital with me. I was starving. My mom's boyfriend sneaked me a bite of Snickers bar and a pickle. It was so good. I wanted to eat so badly.

Sometime after 3 am rolled around and I was 6 centimeters, so the nurses called my doctor in. I'm not sure how far my Dr. lived from the hospital, but I went from 6-10 centimeters in minutes, and it was finally time to deliver this baby. I threw up my pickle and Snickers and tried to focus on my breaths. The nurse kept telling me to breathe and not to push as she was gathering things frantically. Everything started happening so fast. Even faster than the medical staff had anticipated.

I could feel the baby coming. I felt so much pressure I told the nurse, "She's coming, she's coming."

She yelled back, "don't push," but then she looked over and saw the baby's head. "She is coming" the nurse said back as she started pressing buttons and 6 more people entered the room.

A random doctor came in, because mine didn't make it. They said, "take steady breaths and give me a big push." I pushed three times, and my baby girl came rolling out like a bowl of warm jelly. I had been in labor for 23 hours, contracting every 3 minutes, with no food. I was exhausted. I had finally given birth to my beautiful baby girl who was born October 7, 2006. I named her Seven. Seven signifies completeness, perfection, and holiness and she completed me.

She was my blessing.

By day three the nurse said to me that she had never seen a young mother spend so much time with their baby the way they saw me with mine. I never let them take her from me unless they had too. T showed up with his mother on the last day as we prepared to be discharged from the hospital.

We took a few pictures and left and went our separate ways.

We went back to my mom's and we moved again. The house became a zoo—Angel, John, Janice, Drake, and others filled the space. I worked at Starbucks in the airport and supported the household.

Then came the night I was assaulted. I woke to someone groping me—someone I didn't know. I screamed. No one came. I told my mom and Drake. Nothing happened.

I had to leave, but I had nowhere to go. Eventually, my mom demanded money at 12 a.m. claiming it was for bills. When I refused, she kicked me out and threatened to keep my baby.

I went to Drake's. The next morning, I picked up Seven and went to school. That night, I asked a coworker if I could stay with her family. Her name was Ariel.

Her mom let us move in. It was far from school and work, and I eventually had to quit both. I found a job selling vacuums door to door, but that didn't last.

Everything was changing. Too fast.

CHAPTER 12

Statistic

Ariel had a boyfriend, and her boyfriend had a very cute best friend that she introduced me to. Earl was six-foot-two, slim, and had a chocolate-brown complexion. I can't say we had a lot in common other than a love of music. But music was enough for me—music was everything. I was able to express myself through writing and singing.

Earl and I made a lot of music together. Ariel would come by after work and record songs with us too. Earl had a small in-home studio he built himself, using a laptop with Pro Tools and Fruity Loops software for recording and mixing. We used his closet, filled with clothes, shoes, and soundproof padding, as our vocal booth. It became our favorite escape when we weren't working.

Living with Earl was better than living with Ariel or my mom. The downside was being even farther from the city and the bus line—away from both Ariel and my mother. But on the bright side, I was finally stress-free and away from all the chaos my siblings were still enduring. All I had to do was focus on turning eighteen, so I could finally afford a place of my own.

About a month into our relationship, I moved into Earl's mother's townhouse. I couldn't get to my old job anymore, so I started working with Earl at the local McDonald's. I worked the morning shift; he worked the evening. Earl's mother didn't charge me rent—only asked that we help if she fell behind on bills. Most of my money went to Earl and Seven. I remember standing outside Foot Locker at midnight waiting on the new Jordans to drop so I could buy a matching set for the three of us. I should have been saving, but I wasn't.

Earl and I had what seemed like a good relationship. I always seemed to fall in love easily. Eventually, I moved out and went to stay with my grandmother—my father's mother, the only grandmother I really had. I got on the welfare program, which helped me with childcare so I could return to school. By then, it was the tail end of the school year. I went back mostly to try and avoid failing my last semester and began looking into summer graduation options.

It was May, and I had about three weeks left before the year ended. My counselors—both from eleventh and twelfth grade—were determined to help me. They believed I could still graduate with my class, not just through summer school. I soon learned that, after all my hard work and advanced classes, I only needed to pass one final biology test and finish out the month.

Taking the test was the easy part. Getting to school was the real challenge. My childcare paperwork hadn't gone through yet, and my grandmother couldn't watch Seven. Still, the counselors did everything they could to help. They let me finish work in their office and even helped watch my daughter during the school day.

Three weeks later, I walked across the stage with the Class of 2007—graduating in the top 25% of my class. I wasn't a statistic. By the grace of God, I wasn't another teenage dropout. Each student was given ten tickets for the ceremony, but I didn't have ten people to invite. I reserved tickets for my mother, my grandparents, my boyfriend, and my sisters. Earl came with our friends D-Boy and Anthony. My grandmother and grandfather came with Seven. Angel and Janice were in the crowd too. I was so proud of myself. I barely made it, but I made it.

About a month and a half later, my family asked me to stay with my aunt for a few days. Those days turned into weeks, then months. I found out my grandmother was very ill. Eventually, they told us she had lung cancer. She had kept the diagnosis to herself for years. Whether it was too late for treatment or she refused it, I'll never know. What I do know is that she chose to pass away at home, surrounded by family.

She died in October 2007, just before her sixty-seventh birthday. It was hard for everyone. My grandfather went into a manic state and needed supervision. Eventually, he told me I couldn't come back to the house. He said, "It just wouldn't look right"—me living there alone with him. I never understood what he meant, but I had no choice.

I got a job at a shoe store in downtown Atlanta and bounced around for a few months—living with friends, staying in abandoned houses—just until I turned eighteen. That was all I needed. I just needed to be legal so I could put an apartment in my name. Fighting homelessness with a baby, just to keep a job—that year nearly broke me.

On June 11, 2007, I turned eighteen. By August, I had my first apartment. I met a new boyfriend at the studio. He was twenty-one, originally from Washington, and ran his own business with a friend. He helped me apartment-hunt and drove me around the city. He was sweet and completely different from the toxic men I'd dealt with before.

I eventually changed jobs and went back to the airport—this time working as a food prep cook in a restaurant. I let Angel, Erin, Janice, and my niece Esther move in. I knew they needed help, and they helped me with Seven while I worked.

I worked two full-time jobs: food prep and host. My schedule ran from 6 a.m. to 10 p.m. I only saw Seven for an hour most days. It was brutal, but I needed the money.

After six months, Todd and I broke up, I lost both jobs, and I needed a backup plan. God was still with me. I got hired by AirServ Corp, cleaning airplanes. I quickly moved up to team leader. My job was to drive a lift truck to the aircraft, supervise the cleaning, and return by end of shift. I later applied for a supervisor position and started working double shifts to prove myself.

My regular shift was 9 p.m. to 6 a.m., followed by a double from 6 a.m. to 2 p.m. I slept all day, then started over. Eventually, I had to downsize to a one-bedroom. I renewed my lease, but the apartment complex turned into a disaster. I was gifted Gucci purses and belts (don't ask), got into fights, was robbed, and witnessed open gun-carrying and intentional HIV/AIDS transmission. It was time to go.

Only halfway through my lease, I was losing control. No one else in the house was working. I was supporting everyone. Letting my mother move in was a mistake. She was still an alcoholic and addict. She constantly tried to control everything, and we clashed hard.

From my perspective, I'd been on my own since sixteen. I finished school, raised my child, and now supported everyone. I didn't need her running my home.

Still, I loved her. She needed me, and we always just moved on from fights like they never happened. That was toxic, and I know that now.

One day, I came home from work and argued with my mom about not having any money. I told her the rest of what I had was going toward groceries. I laid down to sleep, and just as I drifted off, I heard her come into my room. I heard her open my closet, then go into my coat pocket. Then the door closed behind her.

Half-asleep, I sat up. Something didn't feel right. I rushed to my coat—my money was gone. She'd stolen the last of it. I was furious.

Then she came back—she'd forgotten something. She didn't expect me to be awake. That was the moment I lost it. I confronted her—toe to toe—and told her to leave my house and never come back.

It broke my heart. But it also woke me up. My own mother had stolen from me. And by then, I'd already been robbed by a cousin too. I realized then that it was time for a change.

PART III:

Becoming A Mother

CHAPTER 13

The Engagement

It was the beginning of 2009. Seven was two years old, and it was time for a change. Ariel had moved out of her mother's home and into an apartment on the east side. My lease wasn't up yet at my place, but I needed a new location. I had started trade school and was still working at the airport. Angel and Tanisha convinced me to go with them to enroll.

It was originally Angel's plan, but I ended up signing up too. We all joined the Medical Assistant program—a twelve-month course. At the time, I was juggling full-time work and school. I started looking into apartments near Ariel and found one on North Hairston Road and Memorial Drive. It was a two-bedroom apartment, decently sized for the number of people moving in, and only $450 a month.

Since I was paying all the bills alone, I jumped on the low rent opportunity quickly. My lease wasn't up yet, but the apartments were going fast. I ended up paying nearly triple the rent just to move in—about $1,100 in fees. It was income tax season, so thankfully, I had the money. Still, it was the most I had ever paid to move into an apartment.

Shortly after moving in, I bought a car from the local auction. My job at the airport became more difficult. Initially, we could clock in before the security checkpoint, but new management changed that. Now we had to go through security to clock in.

If you've ever been to Hartsfield-Jackson Atlanta International Airport, you know even the employee lines are long. I caught the earliest bus I could, but it was impossible to get to the D concourse fast enough. My supervisor eventually let me go.

I applied for unemployment immediately and started collecting. Somehow, God made it all work. We survived on unemployment for two years—one year while I finished school and another while I struggled to find work with my new certification.

My small apartment was crammed. Angel and her two kids were there, along with Seven, Erin, Janice, and me. That's four adults and three children in a two-bedroom apartment.

My mom entered a mental facility after our last falling out. She would call me from time to time, and after about a month, she asked to move in. She pleaded with me, saying she was clean and didn't want to go back to her old life.

As scared as I was, I couldn't turn her away. I let her move in. Things were okay for a while, but drama returned. Fights broke out between my mom and Angel or my mom and my sisters. Someone was always fighting.

My apartment was a mess. I was the only one actively looking for work. No one was watching the kids properly. The place was torn up—blinds destroyed, food everywhere, crayon on the walls. My mom was back to drinking and doing drugs. Men came and went.

I hadn't made a fuss sooner for two reasons: they helped me with my daughter, and I hadn't noticed how bad things were. When I was working, I didn't see the daytime chaos. But once I started staying home more, I saw everything.

Eventually, I began focusing on myself and spending more time with Seven. She was funny, energetic, smart, and loving. I remember teaching her to ride her bike with training wheels and taking her swimming at the old apartment. I was trying to reclaim the time I had missed.

Around May 2010, Ariel introduced me—over the phone—to a friend of hers in the military. His name was Terrell. He was 21 and stationed in Italy with the Air Force. We talked daily for about a month.

He seemed like a gentleman, and I liked his energy. Our conversations were long and full of random topics. He told me about life overseas, his military buddies, and how he would treat his future woman. I had only seen one blurry, side-angle photo of him—with waves, sunglasses, and a barely visible face.

I suspected he wasn't attractive. I figured he might be insecure about his looks, but I didn't want to be shallow. I told myself to give him a chance.

In high school, I had already learned the hard way about dating people I'd never met in person. So, I told Terrell I wanted us to start over when we finally met. He agreed—or so I thought.

In July, Terrell flew to Atlanta. I was nervous. I prayed at the airport, "Lord, please let him be attractive."

I stood at the top of the escalator, trying to spot him before he noticed me. I saw a guy in a green jersey and shades. I hoped it wasn't him. My phone rang. It was Terrell. It was him.

He approached me with a big smile. He later told me I was the prettiest girl he had ever talked to. That compliment felt more concerning than flattering. He had been in multiple countries and still said that?

The ride home was awkward. I didn't know how to act. I was trying to be open-minded, but I couldn't fake attraction. I hoped he would grow on me.

We were already calling each other boyfriend and girlfriend. He introduced me to his family, and that part felt easier. His mom was sweet, and he looked just like her. But I couldn't force chemistry.

As the days passed, things got worse. He brought me around his friends, and they would make snide comments behind his back. "What are you doing with this guy?"

I laughed it off, but I was embarrassed—for both of us. Then I met his cousin. He was stunning. I felt even more confused and guilty.

One night, I had a nightmare that Terrell proposed with a silver ring featuring a small center diamond and two tiny side stones. I told him about it the next day and even explained how much I hated the ring.

The Fourth of July came. We planned to go to Stone Mountain Park with everyone—my family, his family, and his best friend. Throughout the day, I noticed him reaching for something in his pocket. I feared the worst.

Every time I saw him go for the box, I stopped him. I was so uncomfortable. How did we go from "let's start over" to a possible proposal?

We reached the top of the mountain. He stood next to me, trying to hold my hand while someone snapped pictures. Then he huddled with his family. I saw the box and walked away. He caught up with me, holding it in his hand.

Before he could say anything, I cut him off. "Just put the ring on."

I was numb. I didn't look at the ring. Everyone wanted to see it, so I held my hand out. No excitement. Just confusion and dread.

He and his family were calling relatives to share the news. I couldn't even look at him.

Later, I sat down on a blanket and finally looked at the ring. My heart dropped. It was *the exact ring* from my dream. I couldn't believe it.

All I could think was: how am I going to get out of this? I didn't want to hurt him—he was so sweet—but I couldn't pretend anymore.

My plan was to wait until he went back to Italy and send him a heartfelt letter. I'd return the ring and his birthday gift and explain that it wasn't him—it was me.

I had no idea how to say it to his face. I just needed time. But as it turns out, things were about to change even more...

CHAPTER 14

The One

Seven's cheerleading practices had started. She had to go twice a
week, and I was a co-coach for the team. We had already attended
one or two practices when, on the third, Terrell asked to come along.
Since we were engaged, he felt he should start being more involved in
Seven's life. I figured there was no harm in him watching rehearsal.

As practice was wrapping up, the football players crossed over
the tennis court fence like they always did, heading to finish their
warm-ups—or whatever it is they do. That's when I noticed someone who looked incredibly familiar. I hadn't been paying attention to
any of the coaches until that moment, but this guy caught my eye. I
watched him walk from one side of the park to the other, then waited
for them to walk back. When they did, he glanced in our direction,
and I stared, trying to figure out if I was seeing who I thought I was.

I wasn't worried about Terrell noticing. He was so far out of my
mind at this point, I barely cared. It wasn't even that I was trying to
flirt—I was just confirming a familiar face. Still, I let it go and waited
until I got home to do some investigating.

I told Terrell I was tired, so he'd go home, then hopped on Facebook. I messaged my friend Dontay, who was the one who'd gotten
me into coaching cheer in the first place. Before I could even ask, I
saw a post he had just made thanking all the coaches and friends
who came to help that day—and right there on the list was the name
I was hoping to see.

His name was Sean Johnson.

He was 5'10.5", light brown skin, athletic build, big brown eyes, and had a gorgeous smile. I remembered him from high school—two grades above me. We had taken a Spanish class together when I was in tenth grade. He was a star athlete in football and baseball, and he dated the valedictorian of his class. He had been my high school crush.

When he graduated, I was volunteering with the school JROTC and was assigned to help during the ceremony. I cried that day like we had been in a whole relationship. The man didn't even know my name. I went home sobbing while Angel, Janice, and Tanisha laughed at me. It was ridiculous—I got a sideways hug at graduation and thought I'd remember it forever. Of course, I forgot about him the moment I woke up the next day.

So four years later, to see him again—it felt like destiny. Same park, same time. I asked Dontay to tell him to come talk to me after the next practice.

That evening, Terrell wanted to come again, but I convinced him to stay home. I wasn't going to let him block what felt like fate. I told him it was hot, that he didn't do anything at practice anyway, and it would be better for him to wait at my place. He agreed.

After practice, Seven and I waited in the car. Sean walked up with a huge smile, clearly happy to meet me. We talked for a while—about what, I couldn't even tell you. We moved to the playground so Seven could play while we kept talking. And then, in that moment, he kissed me.

It was quick, but it happened.

We walked back to the car, still talking like neither of us wanted the night to end. I had two phones—one that Terrell paid for and one I paid for—and both were blowing up. I hadn't even thought about what I was going to say when I got home. And honestly, I didn't care. Terrell would believe anything I told him. Deep down, I think he knew something was up but didn't want to face it.

Sean and I exchanged numbers, and he texted me before I even made it home. Terrell was still at my place when I walked in. He wanted to cuddle on the couch and watch a movie, but I was too busy texting Sean. The truth was, this confirmed everything I already knew—Terrell was not the man for me.

I had never been the cheating type, but here I was. If Sean had been anyone else, I wouldn't have even considered it. But this was my high school crush. A college graduate. Goal-driven. Attractive. Everything Terrell was—but I was actually into him.

I told Sean the truth about my situation. He knew about the proposal, and that I planned to end things with Terrell once he went back to Italy. Over the next few days, Sean and I texted constantly. I tried to play it cool—wait for him to text first, not seem too eager—but every message from him made me smile.

When it was finally time for Terrell to leave, I didn't even see him off. I was just ready for him to be gone so I could finally focus on Sean.

Once Terrell left, Sean was at my place right away. After about a week and a half, things between us were getting serious. That's when I found out Sean had a girlfriend when we met. He hadn't told me. I thought, "Well, I guess we're even." Still, I worried he'd think less of me for what I had done.

Sean started getting jealous about my relationship with Terrell—even though it was over in my mind. I still hadn't officially broken up with Terrell, and I was still driving his car since mine had broken down. I needed to handle things.

I gathered his stuff, including the ring, to send back. But when I looked for it—it was gone. Someone had stolen it. I was furious and stressed. Not only was I breaking up with the man, now he was going to think I sold his ring.

Sean drove me to drop off Terrell's car at his dad's house. I hadn't spoken to Terrell at all. I ghosted him, unfriended him, stopped answering calls. I just couldn't face him. He had been kind, sweet, and thoughtful, but the spark wasn't there. And I didn't want to fake it anymore.

It hurt him more than I thought it would. But I was already too far gone. I was in love.

Sean and I made it official two weeks in. I thought of him constantly. I equated love with butterflies, attraction, and how much someone consumed my thoughts. I was hanging out in the VIP section one night and all I could think about was texting him.

I knew it was too soon, but I texted him anyway: *I love you.*

I didn't expect him to say it back—but he did.

That moment sealed it for me. I couldn't believe this man I'd crushed on since high school felt the same way.

Things got more serious. I started cooking for him—filet mignon, baked potatoes, salad. He'd drive 45 minutes across Atlanta traffic just to see me. He was jobless and broke, but I felt like he was mine.

We started sleeping together and eventually stopped using protection. I knew the risks, but we talked about it. One day I asked, "Are we trying to get pregnant?" He said out loud to himself, "What the hell are you doing, Sean?" I thought it meant he was thinking long-term.

We joked about marriage often—"Keep cooking like that, I'll have to marry you." I thought if I did get pregnant, he'd propose.

Shortly after that conversation, he flipped me upside down after sex. I didn't even react—I was shocked.

Weeks later, I started feeling off. I went to the clinic and was devastated to find out I had chlamydia. I had only been with Sean. I asked him if he'd ever had an STD, and he admitted he'd had chlamydia recently—but didn't finish his treatment or get retested.

I was furious. Disgusted. Hurt.

He apologized, but it didn't matter. Another red flag I ignored.

And yet... I forgave him.

CHAPTER 15

My Escape

It was nearing the end of my lease, and I was ready for a change. I wasn't happy with the way I was living. I wanted privacy—stability. Sean made me crave a normal life, one that didn't involve cramming into a two-bedroom apartment with nearly ten people. I began to feel restless, no longer comfortable with my living situation. I was imagining a future. A family.

I prayed, asking God why I wasn't moving forward. I had finished my certification, but I couldn't find a job. I was working hard and still living off unemployment. My life felt stuck. That's when I heard God speak to me clearly: I needed to let everyone go. He reminded me that He was God—and that He had different paths for my sisters. As long as we were all in the same place, there would be no growth.

That was hard to hear. This had been our normal for so long. I was the provider, the one who kept things together. I didn't know how I was going to make this shift, but I knew I had to. I wanted the life God promised me—whatever that looked like. And He made it clear that nothing would change unless I moved.

My lease renewal felt like the perfect opportunity. I told everyone that once the lease ended, they would need to figure things out for themselves. I hadn't found another place yet, but I was determined. Sean was by my side, and in my heart, this was my moment to finally start a real family, settle down, and create a life I could be proud of.

I ended up moving in with Tanisha, her husband, and my godson. I slept on their couch and spent my days looking for work. Sean visited whenever he could. After about two weeks, I landed a job back at the airport—this time at a restaurant called Nathan's Famous. I worked there for two weeks before finding a decent apartment off Mount Zion Road.

By then, Sean and I were getting closer—and already starting to have problems. I found myself questioning whether I could trust him. I was overreacting, emotional, and unsure.

He went to Alabama for homecoming and didn't invite me. He barely called, barely texted, and at one point stopped answering altogether. I knew something wasn't right, but I was still holding on to the image of the life I thought we'd have. My daughter loved him. I loved him. I thought he loved me. I didn't want drama—I had a child to care for, a new job, and no backup now that I'd moved away from all my help.

Then I started getting sick at work. I felt weak and dizzy. I became obsessed with their biscuits, but they made me nauseous. I couldn't stand for long without feeling like I might pass out.

One day, while taking a customer's order, my vision started to go. I could see the man at first—but as he kept speaking, his face faded into darkness. I saw nothing but blackness and colorful circles.

I felt hot and lightheaded. I reached behind me to touch my supervisor's shoulder and tell her I couldn't see—but before I could get the words out, I collapsed right there at the register. My body hit the floor, heavy and limp. I was shaking, half-blind, unable to move. It was terrifying. I could hear the customer shouting, "She's having a seizure! She's having a seizure!"

No, I'm not, I screamed in my head—but I couldn't speak. My supervisor told the men not to move me, but I begged them to pull me into the back. I was mortified.

They placed me in a chair while we waited for the ambulance. I covered my face as they rolled me down the terminal in a wheelchair. I wanted to call Sean for comfort, but we weren't speaking. Or rather—I was waiting on him to say something.

I sat in the hospital for eight hours. No one had answers. Finally, the doctor came in just as I was being discharged. "The nurse is gathering your paperwork," he said. "And by the way—you're pregnant."

I blinked. "No, I shouldn't be," I said, lying through my teeth.

He looked at me flatly. "I'm not asking," he said. "I'm telling you. So when the nurse brings you the prenatal care paperwork, you won't be confused." Then he walked out.

I laid back on the hospital bed, stunned. I wanted to cry. Sean and I weren't in a good place. My sister was mad at me. My mom was back on drugs. I had no one to call. I finally broke down and called Angel. We weren't close anymore, but I needed someone. I didn't know if I was sad or scared—I was simply confused.

I didn't believe in abortion. And honestly, I didn't expect that to even be on the table considering how this pregnancy came to be. We didn't exactly prevent it.

I rode the bus home in a fog, debating whether to tell Sean. When I got back, I still hadn't decided—but something told me to tell him anyway. Maybe he'd be happy. Maybe this would bring us back together. I texted him: You're going to be a daddy.

He replied: What?

I sent the message again.

What do you mean? he asked.

I told him everything—about work, the collapse, the hospital. Then I gave him space to process.

I don't know what I expected. Maybe excitement. But instead, he blew up. He yelled at me to get an abortion.

I was livid.

I had rearranged my entire life for this man. Moved away from help. Let myself get pregnant. And now he was acting like this wasn't something we planned. I was furious and heartbroken. How did we go from planning a future to this?

Still, when he came back from homecoming, we tried to make it work. But everything had changed. He wasn't affectionate. He barely texted. He took hours—sometimes days—to respond. That's when I found out he was talking to other women.

I remember reading texts between him and one woman while we were apartment hunting. Every morning and every night, he messaged her: Good morning, beautiful. Dream about me. Everything he used to say to me—he was now giving to her.

I didn't even argue. He was supposed to be taking me to work, and I didn't want to fight and risk losing my job. We drove in silence. When I got inside, he texted, asking what was wrong. I told him I didn't want to be with him anymore.

He was confused. But I wasn't.

A few days later, I was pulled aside at work and fired. I honestly don't even remember the reason they gave. All I remember is the overwhelming sense of discrimination—being pregnant and exhausted and now jobless.

My world was unraveling. No job. No relationship. And I was pregnant.

After a few weeks, I gave in and let Sean talk me back into the relationship. I needed a job, and fast. I couldn't afford to show yet. Soon after, I was evicted.

Sean's mother—who was fond of me—let me move into her basement. She didn't see the pregnancy as a mistake; she made the best of it.

I reached out to Mimi, needing prayer and guidance. I was desperate. One of her daughters shared a lead about a security company she worked for. I applied immediately. That same evening, I got a call. Interview the next day. Uniforms by Friday. Training the following week.

But I wouldn't get my first paycheck for three weeks. I arranged childcare with Sean's stepsister, who homeschooled her kids. I'd pay her once I got paid. I still didn't have a car. I had to sign the title over to a tow company because I couldn't afford to get it out of impound.

Sean helped me get around when I couldn't catch the bus. I was five months pregnant when I started working.

Sean's father, who he had a strained relationship with, owned rental properties. He offered us a three-bedroom townhome in Southwest Atlanta. It was better than his mom's basement, but things between us weren't improving.

We made it look good on the outside—smiles and laughter around family—but at home, we were miserable. I kept hoping the version of him I'd fallen for would come back. But he didn't. And he wasn't trying.

Meanwhile, I was pregnant, commuting across Atlanta with no car. I'd wake up at 4 a.m., walk up a hill to the bus stop, ride two trains and a shuttle to get to work. Sean rarely walked with me. Occasionally, he'd drive me up the street—but never all the way.

The commute was grueling. I had to stop working almost a month before my due date. Emotionally, I was worn down. Sean didn't treat me with the affection I needed. And though I now know that even his best wasn't good enough, at the time, I would've settled for the bare minimum—just to feel loved again.

He was frustrated that we couldn't afford our life. I was used to struggling. He wasn't. I was used to stretching what little I had. He saw it all as stress.

He thought I was too needy.

I thought he wasn't stepping up.

We were no longer on the same page.

And maybe we never were.

On July 1st, 2011, after 22 hours of labor, I gave birth to my second daughter—Star. And just like her name, she arrived after a long, dark stretch—shining, beautiful, and bright.

That night started with chaos. I was home alone when my water broke—middle of the night, just me and the silence. Sean was out at the club. I called him, calm but nervous, but he answered with an attitude, unable to hear me over the bass-heavy music in the background. Before I could explain, he hung up. A few minutes later, he called back from the club bathroom. This time, he listened. And when it sank in, he sobered fast.

He sped home with a busted headlight and panic in his chest. By the time he reached our street, a police officer had pulled in behind him for speeding and the missing light. Meanwhile, I was standing in the doorway in a wrinkled dress, holding a towel between my legs like a sumo wrestler—half-laughing, half-terrified. The officer looked between us, probably putting the pieces together. By some miracle, he let Sean off with a warning, and we rushed to the hospital.

We weren't in love, I don't think that we ever were. We weren't even happy. But Star was his first child, and despite everything, I could see it in his eyes—he was nervous, excited, and scared all at once. So was I.

I thought labor would be fast since my water had broken at home. It wasn't. I spent the next 22 hours in agony, waiting for her. Every hour felt like a test of how much I could endure—physically, emotionally, spiritually.

But when she finally arrived, all of it faded. She was perfect. I looked at her and knew instantly: whatever happened between Sean and me, this little girl would never feel like a mistake. She was the most right thing in a season of wrong.

Holding her, I felt peace. I named her Star because even in a sky full of darkness, she was light.

CHAPTER 16

The Breakup

In January of 2012, Sean and I made a big shift in our circumstances. Although we weren't happy with much in our relationship, one thing that remained consistent was our sex life. Don't get me wrong—it wasn't amazing. Most of the time, I didn't even want it. But I was naïve. I had been convinced—maybe even brainwashed—that if that was all we had, I should be giving it to him. I told myself that maybe if I kept showing up physically, he would eventually come around. Maybe one day, he'd love me again. I mean, he obviously enjoyed the sex, right?

But the truth was, we were just existing. Going through the motions. Neither of us was happy.

I was unhappy because I didn't feel loved or appreciated. I knew he didn't respect me—not truly. He saw me as the daughter of a junkie. Poor. Uneducated. Ghetto. And if I'm being honest, I imagine he was unhappy too—frustrated that I was always dissatisfied, that he'd lost his attraction to me, that life didn't look the way he thought it would. And I'm sure he blamed me for that.

Still, I prayed. I hoped God would fix it. That some miracle would happen and we'd be as happy as we pretended to be. I thought time would get us back to love. More than anything, I wanted my daughters to have a father. I knew what it was like to grow up without one.

At first, Sean tried.

He was helpful, attentive—even sweet sometimes. I remember one Saturday in particular, not long after we brought Star home. He heard Star awake. She woke up faithfully bright and early every morning. I could hear him as he got up with the girls, fed them, changed diapers, and let me rest. I laid in bed longer than I had in months, maybe years. And I cried, not because I was sad, but because in that one small act, I felt hope. I thought, maybe this time would be different.

But it didn't last.

Sean's energy for fatherhood, especially when it came to Star, began to fade as quickly as it had sparked. What started as excitement turned into obligation, and then into resentment. His tone grew shorter. He did less. He became more irritable, less engaged. I found myself making excuses for him—maybe he was tired, maybe he was overwhelmed—but deep down, I knew the truth.

He wasn't built for this.

Not this life. Not this level of responsibility. Not this version of me—a woman exhausted, stretched thin, asking for partnership.

It became clear that while I had given birth to a daughter, I was still raising a grown man too.

So, I made an effort. I tried to plan a date night for us. I knew he loved going out, so I put together a nice evening: dinner followed by drinks and a comedy show.

We went to a restaurant that was definitely out of our budget. We laughed about how out of place we looked. He ordered turkey, I got beef. When the plates arrived—fancy, but with barely any food—we laughed even harder. After dinner, we headed to the comedy club.

The night seemed to be going well. But deep down, I wasn't happy. He didn't hold my hand. He didn't walk beside me. There was something missing. I kept hoping—kept trying—but the love I needed wasn't there.

At the club, we grabbed seats in the front row. There was a two-drink minimum, so we ordered Blue MF's—a mix of vodka, gin, rum, tequila, and blue curaçao. Strong drinks. I had just given birth recently, so my tolerance wasn't what it used to be. The alcohol hit me harder than expected, but I was still having a good time.

It wasn't until I stood up to leave that I realized just how drunk I was. Drinking while seated and trying to walk afterward? Not the same. I wasn't falling over, but I had to focus hard to stay composed.

When we exited the club, we realized the valet wasn't retrieving the cars. We had to walk across a gravel parking lot—and I was in four-inch stilettos. A tipsy woman's worst nightmare. I needed support, but Sean rushed ahead of me, focused on finding the car.

I tried to keep up, but I felt like I was being dragged. We walked all the way to the back of the lot—no car. He grew frustrated and picked up the pace again, pulling me along. I was angry now. He wasn't even *trying* to make sure I was okay. We circled back toward the front—and that's when the valet finally called out, "I've been looking everywhere for you, bruh."

The car had been parked up front the entire time.

Now we were both drunk and irritated. I wanted to let it go, but my emotions weren't as easy to control. I told him he was mean to me. He asked why. And somehow, that turned into a full-blown fight in the car.

By the time we pulled into his mother's driveway to pick up the girls, I was missing an earring, my lip was busted, I had bruises on my neck, and I had tried to jump out of the moving car at least three times.

We were still arguing as we walked into the house. I just wanted to leave. I was crying—begging for love, telling him he didn't love me. We managed to get home, but we slept in separate rooms.

The next morning, I sat in the girls' room, my face and body aching, knowing I couldn't do this anymore. I was done.

I still had to go to work. Sean normally watched the girls while I worked, but that morning, he told me I needed to figure something out for *my* child. He'd only keep *his*.

I broke down crying. I didn't know what to do. I called my little sister—not because I expected her to help, but because I needed someone to listen.

To my surprise, she was furious. She said she was coming to get me.

She borrowed a friend's car and showed up with two other people. I had already packed my things, hoping we could avoid any confrontation. I begged her not to say anything to Sean. I just wanted to leave.

But the moment she saw my busted lip and bruises, she lost it. I could hear her yelling, cursing him out. I cried even harder. I didn't want her to think he was a bad person. I still wanted to protect him—for some reason.

After about thirty minutes of her doing everything I asked her not to do, we had all my things packed into the small car. I moved into the two-bedroom apartment my sister shared with a friend. I stayed there about a week, but I knew I couldn't stay long.

Sean didn't reach out. I started focusing on what was next. But in the back of my mind, I still wondered if there was a chance we could fix things.

I had a friend from an old job who helped me get around with the girls. He was an angel—truly. He spent hours helping me look for a car. Eventually, I found one at a buy-here-pay-here lot and financed a used vehicle. (*Note to the reader: Do not do this. Learn from me.*)

Once I had the car, I started searching for an apartment. I found a small two-bedroom not far from my sister's place for $400 a month. Total electric.

And just like that, I started feeling like myself again.

The *me* from before Sean.

The *me* who was proud, confident, independent, and making things happen.

CHAPTER 17

Moving On

After I had my second child, we still hadn't talked about contraceptives—or maybe I just hadn't carefully considered them. I was still stuck in the mindset that if sex was all Sean and I had, then I needed to keep giving it, no matter how I felt, how unhappy I was, or how bad things were between us.

Not even a month after giving birth, before we could even figure out who we were without the weight of each other, we had sex. I was never ready, emotionally, or physically. I felt obligated, and shamefully hopeful. Hopeful that maybe sex could make him love me.

Weeks later, I felt the familiar heaviness in my body. I knew before I took the test. A knot formed in my stomach that no prayer could untie. I was pregnant. Again. Still bleeding from the last emotional wound, and here I was—carrying another child for a man who barely looked at me.

I was tired. Spiritually, emotionally, physically. I wasn't even thirty, but I felt like I had lived three lifetimes. I didn't even tell Sean right away. I just cried and carried it. The weight of the news. The silence. The shame. The same cycle... again.

After everything we'd gone through, this was the last thing I needed. Sean and I weren't even speaking. I didn't know how to tell him, so I had a coworker drop off the test at his house. A few days later, I sent him a text: *"So, you're just not going to say anything?"* He replied with attitude: *"Like what?"* We went back and forth until he asked me to get an abortion. I just cried. I even considered ways to force a miscarriage, but I couldn't bring myself to do anything. I was scared. I felt trapped.

Sean saw me one day getting a ride from that same coworker and got jealous. Maybe at that moment, he realized he didn't want anyone else with me. After that, he started texting again. But soon we were arguing over text, and I went silent again.

I started to shift. I stopped thinking I had to *make* him want me and started realizing that we both deserved happiness—and maybe we couldn't find that in each other.

Eventually, our communication improved. I was still talking to his family, and he and I were texting without tension. As March approached, his lease at his dad's house was ending. Turns out, he hadn't been paying rent since I left, so staying longer wasn't an option. He couldn't afford a place on his own. He was stressed and running out of time.

Despite our improved communication, I knew I wasn't ready for us to be together again. I wanted us to fall for each other naturally—not just stick together because we had kids. Truthfully, I felt better away from him. So, when he asked if he could move in with me, he was shocked when I said no.

Still, I tried to help. I let him keep his TV at my place while he figured things out. Eventually, he got a one-bedroom apartment for $700 a month. I knew it was just a matter of time before the financial strain caught up with him. Meanwhile, I was happy in my own space. I felt like things were finally looking up.

I had my apartment, my car, my children, good health, a job, my own relationship with God, and I was even going to church. I felt *blessed*.

Sean still spent time with the girls, and we had brief moments that felt like a family again—when our eldest graduated pre-K, on the baby's first birthday, at his cousin's events. Soon after, we welcomed our third child, Sean Jr., on August 16, 2012. I went in for a regular checkup. We were expecting Sean Jr to arrive around the 28th of August. To my surprise Sean had already grown to about 8lbs. I was 132lbs myself carrying nothing but stomach.

The Doctor notified me that my amniotic fluid was low and that they needed to induce labor for the safety of my baby. I asked if I could go home first and prepare. She allowed it with a pinky promise that I would pack that bag and head straight to the hospital.

Despite my struggles with sadness and depression during my pregnancies the one thing that always made me happy was holding my babies. I was so ready to see my baby boy. I loved him already. Eight hours of induced labor and no medication later I gave birth to Sean Jr. He was 8lbs and 14ozs 20inches long. He was beautiful.

Despite everything, Sean showed up at the hospital. His family stepped in to help with the girls. And when they placed Sean Jr. in my arms, a familiar mix of awe and anxiety washed over me. He was so small, so peaceful—like he didn't know yet what kind of world he was being born into. And I held him like he was a second chance. Not just for him—for all of us.

Once we were home, just like that, Sean moved back in again.

We were trying—again.

But soon we discovered we had bedbugs. The complex did nothing to help. We lost everything: furniture, clothes, comfort. We borrowed money from Sean's cousins to get a real exterminator. The bugs followed us even after we moved to a new place. We were stressed, in debt, and starting over again from scratch.

Sean decided to apply to the police academy. It wasn't his dream, but he felt pressured. He now had two biological kids and three, including Seven, to think about.

I was still working for the security company, but our new home made the commute unbearable. I applied for jobs at the airport and landed a position at the Duty-Free Store. We were back to faking it—again. Not arguing as much, mostly because we were too busy and too tired.

We moved again once the lease ended, this time into a three-bedroom house on the south side. We had discussed how to manage finances more equally, but Sean was still terrible with money—and worse at listening. I was constantly annoyed. The cycle continued: wake up, drop off kids, go to work, come home. He'd sit on the couch and play video games. I'd cook, clean, parent.

I was exhausted—physically, emotionally, spiritually.

Four years and two kids in, and we were still clinging to something that no longer made sense. I'm sure his family encouraged him to stay, and two of his relatives even pulled me aside to tell me I deserved more. But I didn't listen. I still wanted love. I still wanted the dream.

By 2014, things started changing again. Seven was eight, Star was three, and Sean was two. I enrolled in an online school to pursue a degree. I wanted to make more money and be more independent. I remembered years earlier—when we were homeless—how a woman from our church, a CPA, took us in. She fed us, drove us to service, and even let us stay in her home for a while. She saw something in me and gave me the chance to help with church accounting. It sparked something. Numbers made sense to me. That seed stayed with me, buried under the chaos.

Now, I was finally acting on it.

I started night classes at the University of Phoenix. I was tired all the time, juggling work, parenting, and school—but I kept going. I studied after the kids went to bed. I wrote papers during lunch breaks. I completed my associate degree and even walked across the stage at graduation. But because of financial issues, I never received my official certificate. Still, I knew what I had accomplished.

Two years later, slow to no sex, and I still hadn't found birth control that worked for me, but I was trying. In July 2014, I went in for a blood test to prepare for a new contraceptive. That day, I learned I was pregnant again.

I went home and told Sean. I secretly hoped this time would be different—that he'd finally embrace our family. Instead, he said: "You already know what I want."

Another abortion.

I didn't argue. I didn't cry. I just went quiet.

Part of me had expected it. Maybe even prepared for it. But hearing those words again—like my body was a problem he wanted solved—still cracked something open in me.

But something changed in me after that.

I stopped hoping he would ever change.

And I started choosing myself instead.

I was devastated that he hadn't changed. I asked if he'd consider a vasectomy, since none of the options available to me worked. He refused. Eventually, I scheduled a tubal ligation. I figured maybe one day I'd get it reversed if I needed to—but for now, I was done. Done carrying the weight of his children. Done sacrificing myself.

I spent the pregnancy deeply depressed. I didn't want to be touched. I didn't want to bring another baby into this madness. I was suicidal. I was tired of feeling the way I did. Tired of being invisible. Tired of being a burden. Tired of feeling like I wasn't capable of love. I spent most days feeling like this but some days were just worse than others.

I didn't have the luxury to be depressed though. Only every blue moon. Most often I would be torn up deep down and on the outside, I pretended to have it together for the kids.

On February 28, 2015, I was induced early due to low amniotic fluid-- again just like with Sean. After eight hours, I gave birth to our son, Stephen. It happened the same way. I went in for a regular checkup and was sent to the hospital to prepare for delivery.

But this time, something else was scheduled too.

I cried my way into surgery for my tubal ligation.

I lied face up on the table. Strolling through the cold hospital watching the ceiling lights pass one by one.

Tears rolled down my face.

Me holding my composure.

"Are you ok," the Dr. Asked gently as we approached the surgery-doors.

I nodded yes, silently as I held my breath to keep from wailing. On one hand knowing I'd never carry another child for a man who didn't love me and on the other I didn't want this procedure. I didn't think I was strong enough to never have sex with Sean again. I thought I needed this. But this wasn't just another failed birth control. It was a boundary, a line drawn in the flesh. A final one.

Each time, though my world seemed to be shattered I always found joy in my babies. Family came around more. Things seemed... lighter. One night, we went out to a movie. On the way, I noticed a beautiful bridge near a fountain and said how pretty it looked.

To my surprise, after the movie, Sean offered to take me to the bridge.

It was cold and windy, but I agreed. We walked in silence. I walked ahead as usual. He was complaining, of course, about the cold. I remember thinking, *Why did you offer if you didn't really want to go?*

Then, suddenly, I turned around—and there he was. On one knee. With a ring.

I forced a few tears. I Was more stunned than happy. I couldn't believe he was proposing to me. I wanted to be happy.

But the tears froze as quickly as they fell. The car ride home was silent. I didn't even like the ring.

It was nothing like what I imagined—a planned moment, thoughtful, intimate. This felt rushed, forced. Still, I tried to feel happy. I started planning our wedding.

But nothing had changed. He was still cold. Disengaged. Dismissive.

The day we took our "save the date" photos, I cried the whole way to the studio. I was in full-blown delusion, calling it determination.

One day, as I lay in bed crying, Seven came over and tucked my hair behind my ear and said in her soft, sweet voice.

"It's okay, Mommy. I love you."

That was God speaking through her. *If you stay,* I thought, *this is what your daughters will settle for. This is who your sons will become.*

I was still feeling depressed and suicidal. I hated how things were. I remember the feeling of not wanting to hold my baby because I didn't want him to feel what I was feeling and not holding him made me even sadder. I thought maybe I was experiencing postpartum depression.

I sought therapy. I explained everything, even my concern that I had postpartum depression. My therapist listened and finally said: "I'm really trying not to be biased, but I can't diagnose you with depression. I think if you got away from him, you'd be just fine."

Those words freed me. God was giving me the final out.

I felt relieved. I wasn't delusional. I wasn't sick. I was just torturing myself because I wasn't leaving.

Six months pregnant, I was in a car accident. I was pregnant, caring for three kids, managing a home, and going to college online. I had fallen asleep at the wheel on the way home from work. My car was totaled. By the grace of God, the baby and I were okay.

With no car, I began taking the bus at 4 a.m. to work—while Sean slept. By the time I had Steph I still didn't have a new car. I continued using public transportation.

So, one morning, I searched for bus fare in his car and saw his old phone lighting up. No passcode. God was giving me a sign.

I opened it. Messages from at least six different women. One of them was *her*—the girl from five years ago. He told her he wished he had chosen her.

I shut the phone. Took the two dollars. Went to work.

That night, I said nothing. I needed to think. But when I asked to use his car to go out with friends and he started yelling, I lost it.

"You want to argue? Fine! I saw the messages. You think I'm f*cking stupid?"

He exploded. Started breaking things. Seven ran down, afraid. He yelled at her. That flipped a switch in me.

I blacked out. I grabbed the PS3 I had bought and smashed it. I took off my engagement ring and threw it at him.

I was done.

He threatened not to ask for the ring back. I think he didn't take me seriously. All the times I had left and let him come back. Not this time.

We broke up, but we still lived together, but I began rebuilding. I talked to a coworker who made me laugh and gave me hope.

In February 2016, only a year after Steph was born, I left it all behind. I left Sean, I resigned from my job and made a few other life-altering decisions. Sean never took the ideas of me leaving him seriously so when it was time it did not go well. I had packed up and left most of the children's things because the one thing Sean wasn't capable of was making a house a home. I knew if I took everything it'd be a long time before they had them at his house.

Finally, everything I wanted was loaded and the kids and I got in the car and we left. I never looked back.

PART IV:

Becoming Me

CHAPTER 18

Becoming Me

One unchanging part of the last 27 years of my life has been God—God the Father, The Son, and The Holy Spirit. While my relationship with Him might not have been neat or predictable He was always there. I never stopped praying, never stopped having faith, never stopped trusting Him—even when everything around me was falling apart.

When I was younger, I believed.

At twelve, I gave him my life.

At sixteen, I had faith.

In college I served him.

As I grew older, I learned how to hear him and how to listen.

I learned that you can't just ask God for help and do nothing to aid him. You can't hand over a problem while still gripping it tight.

I use this analogy: our problems are like children. We feel responsible for them. We hold them by the hand and walk them to the altar. We kneel and pray, "God, please help me with this." And He's there, standing with an open hand, ready to take it. Ready to lift the weight.

But what do we do?

We say Amen—and walk right back out with the baby still in our arms. And God watches. Patiently. Lovingly. Waiting for us to let go.

He doesn't shame us.

He doesn't rush us.

He simply waits—ready whenever we are.

Let go and let God.

It took me a while. But I figured it out.

27 years I spent changing who I was to fit an image that Sean had created in his mind. I changed my hair color, the way I dressed. I took out my body piercings. I estranged myself from family and friends. I changed my social engagements.

Don't get me wrong. It wasn't all bad. The physical changes were not good for me but the changes to my community were some of the best changes that I needed for my own growth.

I had my first child at 17 and 4 in total by the age of twenty-six. So, at 27 I had no idea what to think of my body. My physical insecurities were created in this space, the last 7 years of my life, and validated daily.

Finally, I was free.

The time I spent with my coworker was invaluable. I learned how to love myself in this space. I started to become who I was. Finally learning who I was. The funny thing about finding yourself is that you never really know that you were lost until you find yourself.

I moved into a three-bedroom condominium near the house we shared. It was small, cozy, and dark. It did not get much sunlight, but it was mine.

It was ours.

It was new.

It was freedom.

I decorated the boy's room with car beds and painted the girls ceiling in a dark blue and glued glow in the dark stars on it to reflect the night sky. We were all happy.

Sometime after my car accident I financed a car at what should be illegal rates. I had a white 2016 Nissan Versa at 29% interest. It was never affordable, but even more so after I left Sean. So, I let the dealership repossess the car and I bought a Minivan for cash and the kids, and I loved that van.

I enrolled in a Bachelor program at the University and started studying to be a film production accountant. I always modeled and had the dream of acting so, I thought this was the perfect way to get my foot in the door.

I started working as a bartender at a club in my city. I worked Friday and Saturday only and every Monday I would take a few thousand dollars to deposit in the bank.

God could not have created a better circumstance for me. I was surviving off of 48 hours of work per month. This made it quite easy to focus on my schoolwork and children.

Sean and I came to the agreement that he would get the kids two days out of the week. I would drop them off at school on a Monday, he would pick them up and when he would drop them off on Wednesday, I would pick them up. Despite me leaving, Sean still kept Seven along with our other children. I always appreciated that he kept loving my daughter. Or so I thought.

My second year of college I had started dating this guy that my best friend introduced me to. His name was Malik aka Mal. He was kind, had effective communication, and was the perfect gentleman.

All of which I was not accustomed to. I thought I had hit the jackpot. We lasted a year. The funny thing about going without something your whole life is that when you finally get it you are likely to overestimate its value.

Within that year Mal started living with me. At some point he had lost his civilian job, he was a soldier in the National Guard. Living together made the most sense.

Especially, because we were discussing marriage.

He also had a daughter that would stay with us during the summer. She fit in so well with my kids. They even looked alike. We called Sean Jr. and her twins, they were even born 2 weeks apart.

We had a cute little happy family until we didn't.

The agreement for the visitation that Sean and I had with the kids worked for a few years until it didn't.

After I reached the halfway point in my degree program I had decided to commission into the United Stated Army, and I was enrolled in ROTC.

When I was in high school, I participated in JROTC and loved it. I received a letter in the mail back in 2007 with a full scholarship offer to Westpoint Military College but of course I turned it down because I had my daughter and no family to help me.

So, 13 years later the "what if" was right there.

What if, I would have went to Westpoint, and graduated, and Commissioned into the Army.

Well, now was my chance to find out.

And that is why I did it. It was always for me.

My third year of college I left for basic training and when I came back, I lost my job. The club had changed ownership, and they offered me to come back as a server, but I couldn't afford to take that job as it didn't pay a few thousand a weekend the way bartending did.

I didn't know what to do. I could not go to school full time and work full time. Ironically, Mal decided that once he started his new job that it was better for him to live alone for a while instead of staying and helping me keep my condominium.

Instead, he let me move out and into my mother's unfinished basement. My kids crammed into one room on two bunk beds, and I was down in the open basement.

It had no walls and no ceiling.

Just open wood and insulation.

I had to do what I had to do.

Obviously, this is when Mal and I ended.

His priorities were not aligning the way I thought they should have been.

Why leave me now? Of all the times to be present and be available this was the time. Instead, he was ok with me losing my living space and living with my mother. Arguably our relationship was over before he made this decision. I had grown tired of waiting on him to be the ambitious man he sold himself to be. He had dreams and goals but did nothing to achieve them. I was turned off long before I moved into that basement.

Back at school I learned that if I became a resident assistant (RA) that the school would give me a free meal plan and dorm room. I also learned that if I were a Lead RA then I would get two rooms. So, I applied for the position. I was hired as a Lead RA and was awarded to rooms.

I moved into my dorm and the kids slept with me there Wednesday through Sunday. The dorms had one raised twin bed in each room, and a bathroom. I shared common space with two other girls. They didn't mind the kids, and I tried not to be there often. I put extra mattresses under the beds.

Steph and I slept in the upper bed, Star and Sean slept on the mattress that pulled out below me. My sister slept in the other room, and Seven on the mattress that was pulled out below her. It wasn't the best, but we were blessed.

By this time, I had been through about three cars. The minivan broke down; I got a dodge caliber. That broke down as well. I was driving a 2010 Honda Accord with tinted windows, and remote start, but the transmission was going out. I avoided highways and took the back roads to get me to my ROTC program and the kids to school. Despite all the things I could be stressed about, I was happy.

I was optimistic.

I could see the future, the white lining, the upward battle. It would take a lot to get me down because I knew how far I had come.

I was taking twenty-five semester credits and decided to change my major at the last minute to take me down to nineteen credits. The only downside was that the major I chose would require an internship be completed as a graduation requirement. I thought this was stupid because I was planning to be commissioned into the Army, but there was no work around. I had one semester left to go. I started an internship with Enterprise Rental Company.

There was nothing left to do but graduate and prepare for my next adventure.

CHAPTER 19

The Shift

Sean and I were doing pretty decent at the co-parenting thing as long as he thought he was in control. When things got outside of the way he liked it is when things started to go bad again.

My last semester of college, I learned that when I graduated, I would need to live in Arizona at some point for five months to train and after those five months I would take my first duty station at Fort Riley, Kansas.

I wrecked my brain trying to think of the best way to approach the conversation with Sean. I knew how he was. I even discussed it with his mother first hoping she could give me hope that Sean and my conversation would go well. That wasn't the case.

At some point we gathered for a celebration at my apartment where Seans family and mine were all together at once. Not every-one but our immediate family. Sean and I were outside, and I told him that I wasn't sure when but, at some point I will have to move to Kansas temporarily for my first duty station.

He wasn't happy at all.

I mentioned he could move there while we were there so he could maintain visitation.

He said and I won't quote exactly, why would I move there when my family is here?

I didn't say anything else. I realized at that moment we had different ideas of family. My family was my children. His family was his parents, cousins, aunts, etc.

That was the last real conversation we ever had.

He slowly grew more resentful of me.

More hate.

More hurt maybe.

This time was around late 2019. Just before everybody's life changed. COVID hit.

It was the last two months of school, and the school decided no one was allowed to live in housing. My mom's house was not an option.

I had no job.

I had no plans.

I had no resources.

But I had God. I learned quickly that he was already working. That internship that I thought I didn't need offered me a full-time position. I acquired some fabricated check stubs so I could apply for an apartment somewhere. I went back to my very first apartment complex and got a two-bedroom apartment.

I shared a room with my sister, and I put the bunk beds in the other room just like we did at my mom's.

God did it again!

My active-duty date didn't start until November of 2020 so, thank God I had a job to fall back on until then.

I turned our little two-bedroom apartment into a cozy home and school. The sleeping arrangements were tight and there was nowhere to put clothes, but we made it work.

The living room had a futon couch in the center and on the left wall was my desk and on the longest wall, just below our mounted TV was the kids' school desks. I had a little table there for each of them with a cute name plate and teacher name pinned to the wall. A headphone rest. A lamp and a desk organizer to put their notebooks. And a stool that had storage that could be tucked under the table when done.

When you come from nothing, you tend to appreciate the things you have more. What I thought was evident in our struggle the kids really didn't notice until later.

I completed my degree in May and earned a Bachelor of Science in Integrative Studies with a minor in business and unfortunately didn't have an opportunity to celebrate my achievements because of COVID.

But I was proud of me.

As my 5-month training in Arizona approached, I gave my children the option to live full-time with their dad. We went over the pros and cons together.

The pros would be that they would be at a larger house and with their father.

The cons were, and they provided these, that they wouldn't have a quiet space for school. They wouldn't have home cooked meals or snacks. They were afraid to get in trouble. And they wouldn't be able to see my mother or sister because he hated my family.

Obviously, they decided that those cons outweighed the pros.

So, I decided that my training in Arizona would not change our visitation agreement thus he didn't need to know about it.

I left in November, and my mom and sister maintained our schedule. He would pick them up from my house and drop them off the same days as we had done it for years.

Sometime around Christmas, Sean learned that I was away. He was very upset. He assumed because I was away that he should automatically have them full-time. I wish he had been capable. I didn't want him to know it was the children's decision, so I just told him that it was my decision and that if he wanted more time then I agreed that he should go the legal route.

It wasn't a threat, it was a recommendation, and advice for him to have legal rights.

Which he had none.

We were never married.

Georgia is a "mother state" which simply means children born out of wedlock are only legally bound to the mother. The only way to change that was to establish paternity, legitimize, and then take me to court for custody.

He was never responsible enough to put in this much effort into seeing his children.

I always hoped he would try.

Instead, he threatened me. He stalked my home, sending pictures of himself outside of my apartment. Threatened my mom and sister. Illegally used his police badge to gain access to my apartment complex that was gated. It was crazy. He even started to take those aggressions out on the children when they were with him.

I was hundreds of miles away trying to focus on completing the military school requirements which were rigorous at times. Meanwhile, my personal life was on fire.

Sean threatened that when he got the kids on his next agreed upon visit that he wouldn't bring them home. So, unfortunately, I put the ball in the kids court again. Explaining that if they went back, that he wasn't planning to bring them home. I asked if they were willing to take that risk and they weren't. So, I told him, he'd need to take me to court before he could get them again.

A few weeks before my graduation, Seven would experience the beginning of what would be a difficult trauma to overcome. Sean called Seven because she was the oldest, she was the spokesperson for all four of the children. Sean called and Jannette had the phone on speaker while they talked.

Sean asked Seven if she wanted to live with him. Afriad to answer and hesitant to say no she sat there. Janette could see the fear in her face and yelled to seven, *"stop being scared and tell him!"* Seven said softly into the phone, *"no."* He yelled back angry and patronizing, *"well you know what, since you wanna stay with your mom, you ain't never gone be nothing. You are nothing, and you gone grow up to be a ho like your momma. You ain't my daughter. I have a better daughter than you. Don't call my phone no more."*

Before he could finish berating her, Janette snatched the phone from seven as she could hear the terrible things he was saying to her. She exchanged a few words of her own with him and hung up the phone. She consoled Seven as best she could. The kids sat and cried together. Seven pretending those words didn't cut into her soul.

On May 19th 2020, I went to bed excited because the next morning I would wake up, graduate, and begin my journey driving back from military school to see my children that I hadn't touched in 5 months. I wanted to hug them so badly.

When I opened my eyes and started to put on my dress blues I got a phone call. It was my mother. She was frantic. Screaming that they had been pulled over and held at gun point by the police. My sister had been arrested for armed robbery and grand theft auto.

I was filled with emotions.

I was sad.

I was scared.

I was angry. Why couldn't this phone call wait a few more hours.

I was confused. How could she have been arrested for all of this. When did this happen?

Who was going to help me with my kids in Kansas? She was my family care plan.

I cried nearly the entire morning. I could keep back my tears at some points, but I couldn't hide my red eyes. My red face, my red nose. The green vein that pops up on my forehead after holding my breath from trying not to cry. I couldn't enjoy my accomplishments.

I vented and cried to one of my cadre members and I prayed about it. I just laid it all down at the altar. I talked to God and said, well, you must have a plan.

After all, she committed the crime in February and wasn't arrested until the day I was scheduled to come home.

In May.

That couldn't have been anyone but God.

I counted my blessings; said my goodbyes to all the friends I made and hit the road. I had a full 24-hour drive back to Atlanta. It took me three days to make it home.

I pulled up to the apartment.

The kids noticed from the window expecting me a day later. They stampeded out the door, down the stairwell, onto the sidewalk and into my arms.

And this is where our next journey began.

PART V:

The
Final Out

Epilogue

Today is July 18th, 2025. Much has happened—enough to fill a sequel about how we even got here.

Sean Sr. stopped engaging with the children after we moved to Kansas. He made no effort to answer or return their missed calls. After a year passed without any initiative on his part, I made the choice to drive them to him during spring break—I did this for the first two years. I always gave them the option to stay with him the entire time or just visit for a few hours. Of course, I never told him that—it would've only made him lash out at them. And they didn't deserve that.

He's managed to keep in contact with the kids via text to their cell phones. On Christmas of 2024, he did make the 16-hour drive himself to get the children. He ended up stranded for three days trying to get home after driving right into a snowstorm. But during that visit, they met a new baby sister, his daughter with his current girlfriend. They enjoyed the time they spent with them.

My relationship with my mom is still good. I know I'm all she has, and I always want to be there for her as best as I can. Sometimes that is difficult when balancing my needs for peace depending on where she is in life. She was clean from drugs for roughly a year and half. Never sober for too long. When she was clean, she lived with me for a bit in Kansas, but that was rough on the relationships between she and I and her and the kids. So, I bought her a house in GA. We talk regularly and find ways to visit.

I've given up hope of learning who my birth father is but, my father John has been as present as he can be. He keeps up with me. Calls on birthday's or holiday's and promises to send money we usually never see. He also calls if my siblings need money, as I am the liaison.

I have forgiven both of my parents for their poor choices and my unique upbringing. God says, who am I to judge. Plus, forgiveness isn't for the other person; It's for you. I have let the past be the past and I focus on the future and my forward moving. I will, however, remove things and people who do not align with the peace that God has promised me.

Seven is now eighteen. Happy, most days. The last five years have been challengingly filled with abandonment, hurt, and confusion. She spent time in and out of therapy. In and out of her own faith. She left home, explored independence, and eventually came back. She is starting college in the fall but, undecided on her Major. She's looking forward to accomplishing something to make herself proud.

She is wiser now.
She is stronger.
And she is still healing.

Star is fourteen. She masks her emotions when it comes to her father. She wishes he were a better man, a better presence. She carries resentment for his inconsistency and broken promises—but she did enjoy spending time with his girlfriend and their baby during

Sean Jr. is almost thirteen. He is quiet and sweet. He both loves and resents his father. Sometimes he jokes about the abuse, like it was a strange badge of survival. Other times, he reflects on the good things—movies they watched together, food he liked at his dad's house in Atlanta. It's complicated, and he's learning how to hold both truths.

Stephen is ten. He still says he loves his father, even though they have no real relationship. After the first year of unanswered calls, he stopped trying. He made peace with the silence on his own terms.

I am retired from the Army. On the journey of starting a second and maybe third career as a writer and teacher. I am happy. I am in love. I am still making strides toward the future that God has promised me.

I lost nothing worth losing on the way.

I sacrificed a lot-- my time, my trust, my body, my peace, my mental health-- but I gained wisdom, strength, resiliency, and perseverance.

For a long time, I was naïve.

Uneducated.

My story was built on what happened to me.

But now it's about who I chose to become.

I have learned that I am more than just a mother.

Not just a survivor.

I am a woman.

Whole.

Strong.

Free.

And happy!

I am me!

And no one will change that.

Acknowledgments

First and foremost, I give all glory and honor to God—the Father, the Son, and the Holy Spirit. You were my refuge in the storm, my strength in the struggle, and my light in the darkest places. Without You, I would not have survived, let alone found the courage to tell my story.

To my mother, I have forgiven you for your mistakes. Life is a gamble, constantly hoping we're making the right choices and often not. I pray you forgive yourself and find yourself in the present to prepare for the future. Heal and move forward on God's path for you.

To Sean, I have forgiven you for your iniquities. I pray that you can forgive yourself and put the past behind you and focus on your children. That you can grow and become the father that you desire to be and have the relationships with your children that they deserve. Heal and grow for your children's sake.

To my children, thank you for being my purpose. You give me reason to fight, to grow, to rise. Every chapter I live, I live for you. I pray my truth helps you walk boldly in yours.

To my siblings, stay strong. Stay resilient. Stay perseverant. I miss you so much. I love you. I can't wait to see you again and hold you and love you in person. Your story is coming soon, and I hope you let me write it.

To my chosen family, and the ones who stood by me when I had nothing but a dream, thank you for your love, your laughter, and your loyalty.

To the teachers, counselors, therapists, and mentors who saw something in me even when I couldn't see it in myself, your words lingered long after you spoke them. You planted seeds I didn't know would one day blossom.

To every friend who listened to me cry, watched me rebuild, or simply held space for me to be—thank you. You were my safe places.

To every reader who finds pieces of themselves in these pages—I wrote this for you. May this book remind you that your story matters, your voice matters, and your healing is your power.

And finally, to the young woman I once was—thank you for surviving. You didn't give up. You didn't break. You became me.

About the Author

Sharron Taylor is a mother, Army veteran, college graduate, and survivor whose journey from trauma to triumph is as inspiring as it is unflinching. Born in Illinois and raised in Atlanta, GA., she overcame homelessness, abuse, addiction in the family, and single motherhood—while defying every statistic placed on her name.

With a combination of her experience, her undergraduate and post graduate degrees, and a passion for storytelling, Sharron uses her voice to uplift others who've faced adversity in silence. She believes in faith over fear, growth over grief, and purpose over pain.

"I Am Me" is her debut memoir—a raw, courageous, and deeply personal account of a life reclaimed, rewritten, and reborn.

She is currently working on a companion poetry collection, titled: In Search of Love, exploring themes of trauma and love. The book is expected to be released shortly after the publication of this memoir.

When she's not engaged in activities with raising her children, Sharron is doing community service, mentoring young people, writing more stories, and working on new entrepreneurial adventures.

Call to Action

If this book spoke to your heart—if you saw yourself in these pages, or felt inspired to rise above your own pain—I want you to know something:

You are not alone.

Your story matters. Your voice matters. Your healing is possible. We don't heal in silence—we heal when we are seen, heard, and believed.

I wrote *I Am Me* not just to tell my story, but to give others permission to tell theirs. So, I invite you to do the same. Speak up. Write it down. Share it with someone you trust. And when you're ready, share it with the world.

If you'd like to connect with me, learn more about my journey, or stay updated on my next book, please follow me on these platforms:

YouTube: www.youtube.com/@sharronspeaks

Instagram: @sharronb.publishing

Facebook: Sharron B. Publishing

Webpage: https://sharronbpublishing.com

Let's build a space for real stories, real healing, and real hope.